Next Move

Next Move

MY TERRIBLE, WONDERFUL, BIPOLAR LIFE

Troy Roberts

Apprentice
House Press
Loyola University Maryland

First Edition

Casebound ISBN: 978-1-62720-227-5
Paperback ISBN: 978-1-62720-228-2
Ebook ISBN: 978-1-62720-229-9

Printed in the United States of America

Designer: Peter Goodman
Development editor: Lucy Johnston
Promotion editor: Erin Russell

Published by Apprentice House Press

Apprentice House Press
Loyola University Maryland
4501 N. Charles Street
Baltimore, MD 21210
410.617.5265 • 410.617.2198 (fax)
www.ApprenticeHouse.com
info@ApprenticeHouse.com

For Margaret, Clara and Carolyn.

Contents

Foreword

"If we feel our way into the human secrets of the sick person, the madness also reveals its system, and we recognize in the mental illness merely an exceptional reaction to emotional problems which are not strange to us."
—Carl Jung

A surprisingly diverse and illustrious group of people through history have had bipolar disorder. Among many others, Ernest Hemingway, Marilyn Monroe, Carrie Fisher, Edgar Allen Poe, Mel Gibson, Lord Byron, Mark Twain, Jackson Pollock, Graham Greene, Abbie Hoffman, Vivian Leigh, Frank Sinatra, Ted Turner, Edvard Munch, Friedrich Nietzsche, President Theodore Roosevelt, Marlon Brando, Charles, Dickens, the "world's oldest teenager" Dick Clark, Elvis Presley, Bing Crosby, Vincent Van Gogh, Virginia Woolf and musicians Kurt Cobain, Amy Winehouse, Beach Boy Brian Wilson, Demi Lovato and Kanye West have been linked to bipolar.

Were their talents and abilities hampered...or enhanced by bipolar disorder?

Or both?

Bipolar disorder is a paradox in the world of mental health. It can be a paralyzing

affliction, sometimes putting the life of the sufferer in peril through their actions or inactions. Conversely, bipolar disorder can be a wildly empowering condition, permitting some in its grip intellectual or physical achievements most "normal" people could never imagine. Or, on a more down to earth basis, simply allow them to work with a steely, unwavering focus regularly functioning people can only wish for.

The bipolar disorder spectrum affects nearly six million Americans or, according to estimates, more than one hundred seventy million worldwide. Thus, the disorder, counting those afflicted and the people in their lives who are directly affected, could surpass *one billion* people.

This is a true story of one person in that billion.

My goal is to entertain—as I believe my memoir reads like a novel—but to offer a book that is insightful and even revelatory for those looking for perspective about bipolar disorder.

***

I will tell my story through the game of chess. The game of chess is one of the simplest board games to understand. Yet, it is possibly the most complex game ever invented. With sixty-four squares and sixteen pieces of varying abilities per side, the possible permutations for moves and strategies are literally astronomical.

Playing at a high level requires years of experience and superior intellectual horsepower, or at the very least the ability to think ahead in a way that far exceeds the powers of most. The opening moves of chess can set the tone of your game. Mistakes you make early can doom you to failure. And a moment of indecision or, worse, carelessness, can cause ruin. Like in life.

While there have been books about bipolar disorder and books about chess, there is no book that draws parallels between a successful, yet frantic, disordered life affected by bipolar disorder and the profound lessons about life the game of chess can teach us. I have lived such a life and draw upon my experience as a chess Master to offer these life lessons from that perspective.

With this book I have two goals. One goal is to chronicle my manic, blessed and cursed life as a chess Master with bipolar disorder. In the world of chess, I am ranked a Life Master, the highest degree of National Master and just below the ranks of International Master and Grand Master, the highest titles one can attain. Achieving those levels requires a wide and deep array of skill sets. Very few chess aficionados reach those pinnacles.

The other goal is to use the structure and unlimited variations of chess, as seen through the eyes of a chess Master, as a metaphor relating to the unlimited variations of life. The game of chess will be a vehicle to explain, underscore and clarify life lessons, both large and small, as they perfectly parallel the game.

One of the ironies of my life has been the duality of my formidable chess talent and my ability to focus my bipolarity in a way only a handful can. Yet, away from the chess board, I have suffered the frequent contradiction of my so-called chess genius with my erratic and even dangerous personal behavior, often taking outsized risks that constantly threatened to bring the world down upon my head and those I love.

Notwithstanding the genetic component of bipolar disorder to those with the disease, the world in which we exist and the stressors upon us affect the sufferer tremendously. To add to this, for me at least, I was not only saddled with a genetic disadvantage but also plagued by a chaotic upbringing, fostered by instability and surrounded by an FBI Wanted List of unsavory characters, many of whom were close family members.

My mother's choices, at least earlier in her life, ranged from questionable to terrible. Her father was both a mechanical genius and racist rageaholic who had killed many men in war and, yet, in peace could never put down his guns, figuratively and literally. My father was an abusive, sociopathic outlaw, my stepfather a sadistic, perhaps even psychotic criminal, and the succession of men who came into and out of my mother's life, from petty grifters to bikers and Mafia men, meant living in a manic, over-the-top dramatic television series. This human wave of toxicity seared its impression on my young mind as effectively as a red-hot branding iron.

To put it bluntly, I'm damn lucky to be alive, let alone functional. Even more so, successful. Some would say my accomplishments are impressive. From defeating, in match play, Joshua Waitzkin, the chess prodigy who inspired the film *Searching for Bobby Fischer*, to being the force behind the rise of high-end fixtures in big-box home improvement stores that in the last two decades has changed the business model of retail giants like Lowe's and Home Depot. Yet, I have also fallen to profound depths, all of which I will take you through with this book.

***

With this journey, the worlds of chess and bipolar disorder will commingle, often becoming one entity, giving insights not only on the tormented, demented life of bipolar sufferers but offering truths about the lives of so-called normal people, by virtue of the heightened, exaggerated, and often staggeringly honest perspective this malaise imparts.

The other purpose of the book will be overlaid on the first by using the structure and order of the game of chess as a template to understand and analyze what went right and wrong in my life and how others can either be inspired by those lessons. While life can sometimes feel random in its servings of both luck and disaster, chess teaches us that, like it or not, nothing is random. Every choice you make has a consequence, whether it's choosing to walk to the corner market only to find yourself robbed or uttering one small but critical statement or making one seemingly insignificant decision that lands you the chance of a lifetime.

Or brings ruin upon you.

It is the same with chess. Despite the mind-boggling array of choices in the course of a game of chess, while it would easy to adopt a "shit happens" mentality to explain success or failure, the truth is there is nothing arbitrary about chess. Or life.

***

Chess is a symphony orchestra in my head. Literally. I hear music when my game is at full tilt. Music serves as an analogy for many things. For instance, American football is highly-structured and powerful like Beethoven. Soccer, on the other hand, while still

adhering to a definite structure, is much more fluid and freeform like Miles Davis and the Chaos Theory spontaneity of riffing in jazz.

The music in my head intensifies as my attack intensifies. For people who have never played chess, the game looks like two seated people staring at a board with sixty-four squares and thirty-two pieces. Nothing could look more dull, right? On the contrary, in their heads are synapses firing violently. like the ignition systems of two Indy car racers screaming down the main straightaway, two turbulent storms of thought, tension, exaltation...and desperation. Well, for some, that latter emotion is mostly what they experience, particularly if they're playing me. If so then you are experiencing a full-on blitz from the opening gambit. I truly believe how you open sets the tone for the game.

The opening is the first few moves of the game, and this is where you are having to think ahead. Way ahead. If your opening is weak, your game will be weak. In chess, unlike life, there's no time to gain experience during a game. If you start slowly, especially against someone like me, I'll eat your lunch—and breakfast, too. I come out swinging and begin counting my advantages—and your weaknesses—and the hundred ways I can exploit them...after you betray your prowess...or lack thereof...with your *first* moves.

As you make mistakes, and my lead increases, I become like a boa constrictor squeezing the life from his prey, until your mistakes become inevitable and numerous—a preordained, scripted catastrophe. You think two moves ahead, I think three. You think three, I think four. With sixteen pieces each—with varying abilities of movement and attack—as well as the aforementioned sixty-four squares, thinking ten moves ahead is like counting the stars in the Andromeda Galaxy. But it's possible. And if you can only think *a few* moves ahead against me you will lose. That is how I became a chess Master. Sometimes I wish I'd played life the same way.

And sometimes I wish I'd *never* played life that way.

***

I have tried to recreate events, locales and conversations from my memories of them. In order to maintain their anonymity in some instances I have changed the names of individuals and places, I may have changed some identifying characteristics and details such as physical properties, occupations and places of residence.

CHAPTER ONE

The Pawn

"Every pawn is a potential queen."
—James Mason, Chess icon

The pawn is the lowliest piece in chess. It is also the most numerous, numbering eight per side. In the history of chess, a board depiction, some say, of life and war in India prior to the seventh century, the pawn represented the masses, the most economically impoverished of society, the individuals with the least of anything: the peasants. The masses have always been the cannon fodder for kings and countries and have offered themselves wholesale in defense of said rulers and nations, but what of their dreams and aspirations? As humans are wont to do, despite (or perhaps because of) the pressures of great destitution often cause great hopes to well, offering solace to those at the bad end of life's big waiting line, presenting at least the longshot dream of rising above the gravity of lack. In Mark Twain's nineteenth-century rags to riches fantasy, *The Prince and the Pauper*, a peasant's son gets to live as the prince to the king through a few quirks of fate. More famous is *Cinderella*, where a subjugated scullery maid magically triumphs over a dark destiny to find wealth and the love of her life. It happens.

In the opening quote, James Mason—a nineteenth-century chess Master, not the actor from *Lolita* and *20,000 Leagues Under the Sea*—spoke literally of the inherent strength of the pawn: "Every pawn is a potential queen." By running a nearly impossible gauntlet, that is, making it from one side of the board to the other unscathed and thereby reaching the back row of your opponent's turf, the pawn can utterly reinvent itself. With this act of either bravery or recklessness, depending upon how you look at it, the ineffectual pawn becomes a queen, the most powerful piece on the board. The Beyoncé of chess.

This would be the equivalent of a British private making his way to German high command during the Battle of the Somme to become an internecine field marshal...for the Brits. I believe Mason's observation can be extrapolated to the game of life. The rise from nothing to everything...or at least something significant. Defying the odds. The little guy not only surviving the system but soaring. Icarus without the vulnerability of wax.

Or being either smart or lucky enough to fly in overcast.

Giving the little guy hope is an important psychological mirage the rich and powerful depend upon to keep the poor in line. Through history, the poor, like Bon Jovi said, are often *"livin' on a prayer."* Thus, the pawn's dream—in chess at least—is to become the most powerful piece by traversing the board from one side to the other and, thus, change its destiny.

The common reverse of that noble aspiration is that most people never rise to great heights but rather remain pawns, often being manipulated by others, whether it's politicians, bosses, co-workers, friends, family, or even circumstances. Those are the pawns you lose early in the game. Usually, these pawn's dreams, at least in real life, are simply to survive. The pawns in chess are merely removed from the board and serve no other function than to tally your wins or the other guy's defeats. As for those flesh and blood unfortunates, when they're metaphorically removed from the board, while they continue to exist, their lives are truly borne of quiet desperation and the death of dreams. Those players go into a sort of limbo as the game continues.

Such was the life of my mother, Georgia Noonan.

***

Georgia began with little to no power. As she moved into her teens, she could not seem to change her destiny no matter what she tried. However, her choices were often flawed, to say the least. She never really made it to the other side of life's chess board. Georgia, a self-confessed "wild child," grew up in an abusive home on the outskirts of Savannah, Georgia.

Her mother, Carol, was a professional person who had some odd beliefs about child rearing. She was in college for much of Georgia's childhood but, ironically, eventually graduated with a master's degree in child education. Despite her advanced degree in dealing with children, she tended to treat Georgia harshly, for instance, refusing her even a pittance to have fun with her friends. Georgia didn't ask for a lot. One time, she desperately wanted some stylish Capezio dance-style shoes that were all the rage, so she could fit in with her friends, but her mother wouldn't part with the few dollars she could have easily afforded to get the shoes in the late forties. Aside from tight, her mother was also a devout Christian Scientist, which embarrassed Georgia to no end for its odd belief system, but when Georgia's younger brother, Charles, was stricken with what seemed to be a severe autism, she prayed over him and eventually effected a transformation in the boy to what most considered normal. A miracle? Perhaps.

The Noonans had four kids: my mother was the eldest, Charles was 22 months younger, Troy (yes, I had an Uncle Troy) was seven years younger, and John was ten years younger.

Georgia's father, Edward Noonan, was a stubborn, self-actualizing individual who served as the millwright and chief mechanic at a nearby corrugated box factory. Ed, later dubbed Granddaddy Noonan by my little sister Marie and me, was a manly man who hunted, fished and repaired just about anything with moving parts. He was more or less a self-taught engineer who had taken some courses in engineering and, when they began appearing on the market in the fifties, a devoted

Volkswagen mechanic. Ed also believed a firm hand was important in both marital relations and child rearing, so he beat both Carol and Georgia as if they were recalcitrant farm animals.

Home life was hard on Georgia, partly because of the chemistry with her parents, her rebellious streak and the abuse waiting for her at home, having the crap kicked out of her. By sixteen, Georgia had had enough and fled to Atlanta. To what she was fleeing, she didn't know, but she hoped it would be better circumstances than what she had known growing up. When you rebel at such an early age, you generally don't yet have the tools to cope with the "real world," so this break from the adults in her life, however cruel they were, was a leap of faith she'd prayed was going to work out.

A friend there had just given birth, so Georgia moved in and traded child care for room and board. Six months after arriving in Atlanta, Georgia's friend announced that her brother was about to get out of prison and coming to live with them. The brother had done a stretch for dealing narcotics. Unfortunately for Georgia, her break from the frying pan of home dropped her into the fire with the arrival of the brother.

Georgia's first impression of Donald Roberts was that he was handsome and polite, which at first was enough, since he seemed to treat her reasonably well. He was also five years older which made him quite worldly to the small-town teenager. But Georgia's rosy glasses didn't stay on long. Mr. Roberts charming early impression masked the truth that he was a morphine-addicted, alcohol-sotted, sadistic, petty criminal as well as a serially unemployed troublemaker who never seemed to meet a job he liked—or that liked him. Other than that, he was a model citizen and stand-up guy.

Donald soon had Georgia in his thrall. After seducing the sixteen-year-old girl,

Donald the hophead began pimping out Georgia to pay for his drug habit. Other than his embrace of morphine, Donald also had a taste for liquor and the more the better. When he wasn't pimping out Georgia, he was drunk and beating her. In between her bruises and split lips, people told Georgia that she looked a lot like Elizabeth Taylor. It was small consolation knowing that soon she'd get the stuffin' knocked out of her and, once again, look more like one of Rocky Marciano's opponents than the star of *Father of The Bride*. Yet while Georgia had left her parents behind because of the beatings, she took Donald's beatings, because, in her own words, she felt worthless and that, just maybe, she deserved the abuse.

Anyway, she admitted to herself and others that she was in love with Donald the addicted miscreant, so that somehow made the bad medicine go down a little easier. What Georgia did not know then was that she had inherited bipolar disorder from her sadistic father Ed and this condition made her impulsive and depressed a lot and, thus, vulnerable to manipulation, first from her father and, now, from her morphine-enthusiast paramour.

Donald eventually took Georgia away from Atlanta, first to New York City, then Detroit. They got married when she was old enough, and soon Georgia found herself pregnant and in a life quite different but just as bad for other reasons than her life in Savannah had been. Before her pregnancy, Donald and she shared a love of the drink, but once she knew she had a bun in the oven she quit drinking. Research back then on liquor during pregnancy was inconsistent but there was a school of thought that it was not recommended. My mother, despite her tender age but to her credit, erred on the side of caution.

Life in Detroit was uneventful but, by then, with a child on the way, Georgia realized it was going to be difficult given Donald's uneven relationship with employment and sobriety. When she was seven months pregnant, Donald did something that would change the lives of everyone around him. What he did could easily be considered comical if it hadn't been so tragic for the young woman with child who needed him as much as did that unborn baby. The event merely cemented the fact that Donald Roberts was a real piece of work.

Despite having more going for him than he seemed to realize, like natural good looks with wavy brown hair and an intellect that was profoundly belied by his actions, Donald had spent his first quarter century finely honing his skills at snatching defeat from the jaws of victory. So, with a child on the way and desperately in need of feeding his real concern, his narcotics habit, he devised a plan to get his hands on some badly needed gelt.

Unfortunately, his carefully crafted scheme had one large hole in it. One day, Donald walked into a restaurant he had frequented for some time. Being a regular, everyone who worked there recognized him and even knew him by name. On that morning, the waitress likely smiled at him and offered, "Nice to see you again, Don." Only, that day, he didn't order ham and eggs or even a cup o' joe. Rather, he pulled out a gun and demanded all of their money. They handed it over, and he fled. Needless to say, identifying him to the police was as simple as, "It was Don Roberts who did it," and Donald quickly found himself a guest of the Detroit police department. Most states, and the State of Michigan was no exception, frown on obtaining loans at gunpoint so they held him for trial with the intent of putting him up in a five-by-eight concrete studio apartment to ponder his bad deeds.

With Donald in custody, a pregnant Georgia had to make a quick decision to protect herself and her baby and moved in with her grandmother who lived in Detroit. While he awaited his trial, Donald knew he would soon likely find himself a guest of Jackson State Prison, famous at one time for being the largest walled institution in the world. Donald was looking at a five-to-ten stretch for his little misfire at the diner, which would give him the time he needed to contemplate either his misdeeds or his plans for his next robbery.

Regardless of what he was thinking, two weeks before moving into his new dorm room, Donald had yet another milestone to deal with: he was now a father. Donald's haphazard and slapdash approach to life had produced yet another victim. On October 24, 1956, his son was born. Georgia was my mother and Donald the ex-con, morphine-loving alcoholic, about-to-be-imprisoned wife beater was my father.

I was born of conflict. It was perfect.

CHAPTER TWO

The Bishop

"A man who is willing to commit
suicide has the initiative."
—Boris Spassky, World Champion

The bishop's only moves are angles. The bishop moves diagonally to every other piece and has no restrictions as to how far he can move. This makes him a bit shifty in that he can come completely out of left field and cross the entire board to do you damage. The bishops are also identified by either their affiliation with the king or the queen, depending upon which side they start on. Ralph Juliano was a king's bishop who worked the angles of life.

I acknowledge that my old friends—chess and chaos—have one thing in common, *conflict*. That was my life growing up: unending conflict. Adding to the rogue's gallery of conflicted individuals in my life, Ralph Juliano ranked quite high in his ability to upend the lives of those around him, not to mention his own. Ralph, like my father, was a petty criminal and low-life, who gambled everything from cash to the well being of everyone he touched.

With her husband in prison, my mother needed to pay the bills, so she managed to find a job as a waitress at the Peter Pan Restaurant near the Detroit Race Course, a horse track in Livonia, a western suburb of Detroit. My great grandmother Nana babysat me while mom slung hash. The Peter Pan was a hangout for jockeys, and being an attractive young woman, it wasn't surprising that one of the jockeys developed a thing for my mother and worked hard to get her to reciprocate his feelings. She just wasn't interested, and it wasn't simply because he was eight inches shorter than her. They had no chemistry, plain and simple.

However, he did have cash and finally came up with an arrangement to get her on his arm: he'd throw her fifty bucks a date to simply be his escort and show up with him at places he frequented. This filled the small man with pride that he'd managed to hook a hot looking armpiece and could show her off. My mother got fifty clams (she extended no untoward benefits to him by the way) which was a lot of dough back then. It was pretty much enough to pay the rent. After the abuse she had taken from Donald at least the jockey treated her well, and she made some good jack in the process. One night, he took her to a snazzy dance at a local hotel and her life changed.

As the ballroom filled with people, my mother and the jockey made their way onto the dance floor and swung to the sound of big band music. They were having a good time. For a moment, my mother forgot she was being paid to dance with her diminutive beau. Then, she caught a glimpse of the "most handsome man" she'd ever seen, as she would later describe him to me. With the dark, Italian good looks of Ray Liotta's character Henry Hill from *Goodfellas*, this guy was the sharpest, most dashing man my mother's tired eyes had laid a gaze upon.

When the jockey went to the men's room, my mother grabbed a matchbook, quickly scrawled her name and work address on it and boldly handed it to the sharp man. At this point, having been through hell with Donald, the hop-headed, alky wife-assaulter, she figured taking a chance like that was child's play. So, smitten by this irresistible stranger and, perhaps, so desperate for a life better than she'd had so far, my mother dreamily told friends, "I've met the man I'm going to marry." It was a line torn right from one of the movie tabloid magazines of the time but to Georgia it was a possibility. At least it was in the starry moment she uttered it.

But as the days turned to weeks and no call came, my mother gave up hope, sighed and mentally moved on. The sharp guy at the dance was just an illusion to the lonely, lovesick young woman looking for both companionship and a father for her son. Amazing moments that have a full arc of emotion and complete, satisfying storylines really only happen in the movies. In real life, they just end in disappointment.

But, then, life has a funny way of surprising us. Three weeks after she handed him the matchbook, the sharp-looking man walked into the Peter Pan Restaurant to my mother's astonishment. There was a self-assuredness about him that disarmed my mother, on top of his striking looks. The other waitresses had heard about the mystery man. Like the story of Bigfoot, they'd long since chalked him up as a tall tale my mom told to impress them. But yet...here he was.

"Let's go," he said to my mother, "we're gettin' outta here."

My mother didn't know what to say to the man she didn't know from Adam.

"Uh, I can't. My shift's not over. I..."

"Yeah," he said, coolly flicking his gold Ronson with James Dean assuredness and lighting a cigarette. "It's over now. And you're not comin' back. You're done here. C'mon."

The bluntly romantic moment was right out of a George Raft or Bogart film, and the certitude in his outrageous take-charge Italian attitude shorted Georgia's brain circuits. Sure, he was clearly another bad boy and while that was almost irresistible to the impressionable new mother, his style could not be denied. And on top of being a bad boy, he was a bad boy *who wanted her*. Now.

Right out of a movie, she tossed off her apron, walked out of the Peter Pan Restaurant, got in Ralph Juliano's shiny Caddie, and off they went, never to look back.

***

With Ralph's heart fluttering assurance to "take care of you," my mother felt she'd finally found the man of her dreams, and they laid plans to be married, just as she'd predicted. Having swept her off her feet, Ralph told Georgia he had business out West, so they decided to hit the road and get hitched on the way. With their first stop in Baltimore, Ralph's home town, they decided that an eight-month-old baby would be a buzz kill on a road trip, so Ralph asked his Uncle Jake and Aunt Peggy if they would take care of me while they crossed the country to institute Ralph's plan to cash in on the horse track circuit.

Unfortunately, Uncle Jake and Aunt Peggy were ill-equipped to deal with a toddler given the busy operation they were running at their apartment (much more on that later) so Aunt Peggy suggested to my mother that she give me to her daughter in Jacksonville, Florida, for the few weeks the newlywed couple would be on the road.

They followed that lead and dropped me off with Aunt Peggy's daughter, Shirley, in Jacksonville and hit the road. Shirley and her husband had no children and were happy to see to my well-being for a few weeks. In short order, Shirley fell in love with me. It turned out my mother and Ralph would be on their sojourn for more than a year, giving poor Shirley plenty of time to fully invest her heart in me and feel like a mother. Ralph and my mother took to the open road as vagabonds, following the racetrack circuit from Chicago to California.

Their first stop was Chicago, but then Ralph said they needed to get to California as soon as possible. Santa Anita, California, was where the action was supposed to be, so they planned to get married and take their honeymoon on the fly as they headed to Southern California.

Along the way, Georgia began to realize what she'd gotten herself into with Ralph Juliano. He turned out to be quite the heavy hitter on the bottle. Having experience with Donald's excesses, she soon saw the same pattern of drunkenness in Ralph. But by then, she was stranded on the back highways of the United States with yet another alky, and she did her best to ride out the situation. But there were moments that stretched her ability to cope.

Georgia quickly discovered that Ralph's associates were generally a pack of assorted lowlifes and bottom dwellers. My mother never got used to living on the dark edge where Ralph took her, no better illustrated than when Ralph decided to pick up a hustler buddy in Chicago to share expenses on the trip to California. In Oklahoma City, the hustler asked to stop at a pharmacy, presumably to get some medicine. It was medicine all right. He paid the pharmacist extra to craft a potent concoction of cough syrup that he and other addicts liked to get high on. What happened next would be a caution to perhaps check and see if your pharmacist was both qualified and understood what they were mixing up.

Back in the car, the grifter swilled down the potion, went into convulsions and died on the spot, right in front of my mother. This was the first of many second thoughts she began to have about her new husband and those in his orbit.

Aside from people dying more or less in her lap, the road did give the couple a chance to get to know each other. For my mother, it was nightmarishly revealing. During their extensive time on the road and, later, in California, Georgia came to know the real Ralph, a raging, uncontrolled alcoholic.

Despite her misgivings, they got married in Tucumcari, New Mexico, finally making good on her prediction to her friends. Only she wasn't quite as enthused as she had been some months earlier. But she was in for a pound, and they made their way to Southern California where they could get some sun and Ralph could earn from his skills as a race track tout. Ralph really liked being a tout and was, by all accounts, a good one.

Touts sniff out a sucker who bets big and use a tried and true scam: they confidentially give the mark a "secret tip" that he knows a certain race is fixed, activating the mark's greed glands on a sure thing. The tout will tell him that he will give the sucker the dope on the fixed race if he promises to cut the tout in for a percentage of the winnings when the sucker places the bet with his own money. The sucker can't get to the window fast enough, confident in the knowledge he's got the inside line.

The beauty of the scam is that if the horse happens to win the tout gets a decent percentage of the take and a mark he can work again. But if the horse loses, it doesn't matter as it was the sucker's money and "something happened." It wasn't the tout's fault. If the tout's lucky, he doesn't lose his mark, but if the mark cools to him he just moves on to the next chump. It's a win/win for the tout and a win/lose for the victim.

If the tout happens to be a good handicapper and can consistently pick winners the tout can string a whole succession of suckers for more bets and keep cashing in. The variables can include a myriad of factors such as the condition of the track, the weather, who's getting medication, the jockey, the distance, etc., and the insider's gold: who might be holding a horse back or if a race really *is* fixed—strictly illegal but done all the time.

These skills and intel would come in very handy for the successful tout. Ralph would troll for "clients" at the hundred dollar windows. Back then the windows that trafficked strictly in Ben Franklins was only for really high rollers. Ralph was very good at picking gullible people and winning horses.

When he wasn't getting hammered.

And when he was it was sometimes a doozy.

The topper to the trip was when Ralph went on a month-long drinking binge and my mother and he ended up flat broke because Ralph was too incapacitated to tout at the track while distilling their available cash into booze. Once he sobered up, penniless and desperate, Ralph sold the tires and wheels off the Cadillac, so they could at least eat, and no doubt buy more hooch. With the once proud Caddy on cinder blocks, he eventually sold that too and used some of the take to send my mother back to Baltimore and the safety of Uncle Jake's house.

Oh, and the other highlight of the trip? Georgia discovered she was pregnant again.

CHAPTER THREE

The King

"Good players develop a tactical instinct, a sense of what
is possible or likely and what is not worth calculating."

—Samuel Reshevsky, U.S. Chess Grandmaster

The king is arguably the most powerful piece on the chess board. I say arguably because the king seems relatively frail. He's guarded by the lives of the other pieces and can only move a single square at a time. However, his survival is the core of the game. Take out the other guy's king and you win. The king is the locus of chess, the piece everything else hinges on. Thus, I can argue he's the most powerful piece, the cornerstone of the game. The king, by virtue of his importance, causes everyone else to do his bidding and protect his life. The game exists to further the interests of the king and no one else. Queens come and go but the king is the name of the game, baby.

Castling the king is a move designed to protect the king. If certain parameters are achieved, generally not moving certain pieces until the castling occurs, the king's rook and the king may exchange places, literally, by leaping over each other to put the king in a more secure position. This is the only time a "jumping" move is allowed in chess for any piece other than the knights. It attempts to guarantee your king's lineage perpetuates, at least until you can kill the other guy's king...or he resigns just before you do so. Resignation is preferred in the civilized game of chess as bloodshed is so untoward.

Frederick Juliano, a.k.a. Uncle Jake, was one of twelve children, born in 1906 in Highlandtown, one of Baltimore's working-class neighborhoods. Just east of downtown, Highlandtown was typical of East Coast melting pots back then, with large populations of Polish and Italian immigrants looking to taste the American Dream. Uncle Jake's dad owned a bar and from an early age Jake decided he would never be one of those "lunch bag men," as he so contemptuously referred to the endless line of working stiffs who filled the stools from dawn to closing, on their way home from their mostly factory jobs. Uncle Jake wanted to be like the other half of the patrons, the sharp guys with the ever-present gorgeous female eye candy and big bills they peeled off like lettuce. Agreeing with Henry Hill in *Goodfellas*, Uncle Jake believed the idea of living any other way was just nuts.

By the time he was seven, Uncle Jake discovered skimming his dad's till was a helluva lot better than an allowance, and he and his buddies would catch the trolley to where all the action was: Pimlico Race Track. Outside the turf club, he would always find a three-card monte game or just bide his time pitching pennies until enough suckers had congregated to start one. When they got tired of taking the money off marks, they'd deftly reach into jackets and pants and lift wallets and spare change. Uncle Jake sensed money like a divining rod in a drought; he could always find it.

Not interested in wasting his time on any sucker deal like a formal education or regular job, Uncle Jake left school in the third grade, around the time his father busted a pool cue over his neck, leaving him permanently disfigured. Jake's father never spared the rod. Once, after catching Jake with his mitts in the bar's register, he marched Jake over to a red-hot stove and pressed the child's hands to the fiery iron. With a Mark of Cain that he would carry the rest of his life, Jake would be much more careful about stealing the bar's receipts in the future.

He lived his mantra – *I don't wanna be no lunch bag man!* – by never taking the conventional path for a career. While it wasn't necessarily easy, he was never not his own man, even as a child. At a very young age, Jake learned that in order to avoid being a lunch bag man, you had to be "sharp" and constantly "work" every situation to your advantage. Even the smallest hustle was a victory and a stepping-stone toward getting sharper and sharper. "Sharpness," in all of its respects, grew stronger as his philosophy, just as his disdain for conformity grew.

As teenagers, Jake and his pals decided the small-time grifts at the track were for chumps and took it up a notch by rolling drunk, freshly-paid sailors as they staggered out of the bars at Fells Point. When Uncle Jake was seventeen, he fell in love with Mary, a beautiful Italian girl with long lashes, full lips and coal black hair. Uncle Jake's true love came from a nice family and, knowing Jake and his illustrious reputation, Mary's brothers fought hard to keep him away from her.

It was in vain.

Jake had a crush on her and she on him, and they both went against the wishes of her brothers as she persisted in seeing Jake. She offered to do anything for him and, being a sentimental fool, he got her a job at a brothel and collected a piece of her take. The brothers' instincts about Jake had been correct. Jake first took her virginity, then her innocence, then her humanity. He methodically transformed her from first his own private whore to simply a commodity, regularly pimping her to his friends.

Ultimately, after developing and "proving" her skills, he sold her to a whorehouse in Havre De Grace, a community northeast of Baltimore at the mouth of the Susquehanna River. Only years later, much too late, did he realize that he had really loved the girl. Was that a change of heart for a sociopath or did he muse about that for some effect? Who knew? His actions would never have betrayed any heartfelt feelings.

Around the time he arranged for Mary to take her out-of-town position, the government in its infinite wisdom decided to pass the Volstead Act, a.k.a. the Eighteenth Amendment to the Constitution, between late 1919 and early 1920, making sure thirsty troops returning from war in Europe had to drink illegally. It also made sure that the nascent seeds of organized crime had incredibly fertile soil in which to sprout and spread.

Recognizing opportunity, Jake and his boys got into the growth industry of bootlegging. It was in this field Uncle Jake would find employment with the fastest growing and most successful corporate institution in the United States: the Mafia.

***

Chess has many rules. The structure of chess is designed to create order and allow for invention and even brilliance. Chess helps define the raw intellect and strategic acumen of a player. But, again, the system operates within specific strictures to ensure a so-called level playing field. All things being equal, it becomes the task of the player to assess the seemingly infinite possibilities and make your choices, particularly when every move by your opponent creates a new universe of options. This is the beauty of operating within a system of known rules. Everyone has the same chance before any moves are made.

This is a lovely thought if only it could be translated to the real world. Sadly, it isn't. While most people go through life playing—mostly—by the rules, there are those in society who find the rules a burden and write their own. These are the outlaws, the renegades, the unrepentant individuals who rig the game for their own benefit, at least until society judges them lawless and has them cease their activities, punishing them or causing them to stop what they're doing. This generally comes through fines, imprisonment or, sometimes, death. But there are those who never quite stand for a reckoning, they somehow cheat the hangman and make it all the way to the opposite side of the board with nary a slap on the wrist.

Jake had some run-ins and did a little time. As a guy like him might say, he could do time standing on his head. Jake, almost from the get-go, was a guy who felt societies rules were for others, suckers or even lunch bag men. Not him. Frederick Juliano played by Jake's rules and that was that. But karma sometimes has an odd way of making entries in the big ledger. For Jake, while imprisonment might not have been a big deal, there were other ways the Universe works to get some people's attention.

One night, Uncle Jake's luck took a strange turn. On a bootlegging run from Hagerstown, Maryland, to Baltimore, he got in a high-speed chase that devolved into a gun battle with police. He ended up crashing his delivery truck. The driver and guy in the middle died. While Uncle Jake survived, he lost a massive chunk of flesh from his shoulder down his arm and was marked for the rest of his life with the terrible canyon-like gouge. He also hurt his leg badly and limped the rest of his life from his injury.

On top of the physical trauma—eight months in Johns Hopkins got him back on his feet—he was transferred to the state pen on Guilford Avenue where he did seven years. The good news was the seven years showed his mob superiors he could do time without ratting anyone out. When he was let out, his cousin, a made guy, got him set up in his own operation. His cousin owned an Italian restaurant, and while the mob kingpins liked Jake and felt he was a decent earner, he was seen as a little bit of a loose cannon.

Worse, he drank too much. In the Mafia version of HR, it limited his ability to rise in the ranks. Jake was a "friend" of the mob but was never "a friend of ours," a huge distinction in Mafia argot. This meant, if Jake wanted to do anything, he would always be on a short leash to his mob overseers. Despite his limitations, Jake did experience some good fortune and sort of benefited from being at the right place at the right time.

The factors working in Jake's favor to allow this good fortune were few but important. It was the thirties and Prohibition was ending, thus weakening the grip the Mafia had on Baltimore. On top of that, some of the Italian mobster dons like Pasquale "Patsy" Corbi had gone to prison for murder a decade earlier, coupled with the rise of the Jewish Mafia under Moe Cohen, who worked for gambling kingpin Meyer Lansky. While the Jewish Mafia made inroads in Baltimore, and although the Gambino-run mob structure in the area still controlled most of the vice, the Mafia bigwigs were far more focused on other territories, such as New York, Jersey and a growing presence in the Midwest.

These events conspired to create a power vacuum that Jake stepped into. While technically a mob town, in reality, Baltimore was more or less an open city because of a lack of Mafia command-and-control, so Jake could cut a fat hog and not really answer to anyone. This was practically unheard of, especially for a guy who wasn't even made.

After his stint in jail for the botched bootlegging run that ended in the crash that disfigured him, he settled into more conventional ways to make money, some even legitimate. One avenue he pursued was real estate, and he used some of the money he'd stashed to buy a large, stone-facade row house he converted into a sort of headquarters and rooming house. In a neighborhood called Mount Vernon, 1315 North Calvert was three blocks from Penn Station, across the street from the old Mount Royal Hotel, with the Belvedere Hotel only four blocks away.

His purchase of this particular property was no accident. Since Uncle Jake and his crew were hustlers, they could keep their fingers on the hustles ongoing at the hotels or quickly hop over to the train station to spread their grifts to Philly or D.C. Calvert Street was Uncle Jake's O'Hare Airport, a perfect hub to cover a large territory. And, like any other seasoned professionals, their methods employed great precision, timing and creativity. Uncle Jake was a guy who recognized opportunity and even used the privations and efforts during WWII to find ways to make money. Had anyone else been labeled a war profiteer, they might have been ashamed, but Jake likely would have laughed and agreed. At least he was no lunch bag man.

One of his scams during the war consisted of posting men along a route where pigs were literally herded along streets between the stock yard and the slaughterhouse. As the pigs were run down the street, his men would snatch some of the participants and sell them to local butchers. Jake was both an innovator and clearly not above the pettiest of contrivances to make a buck.

Jake cut a particular figure in the neighborhood and the larger community of law breakers in general. Of average height and a beefy buck-ninety, Jake epitomized the swarthy southern Italian with a prominent nose, olive complexion and hair carefully slicked back without a strand out of place. He almost always wore suits as if there was never a day of leisure or relaxation to allow for more casual attire, and those suits often were draped with only the best cashmere coats and topped with the best quality fedoras. Simply put, he was the quintessential mobster out of Central Casting. He also prided himself on his fine iron, usually picking a new car every year or two, at the outside, mostly Buicks, although one year he tried a Lincoln, then went back to General Motors the next year.

Jake's parents were from Rome and Naples, so being in the kitchen was baked into his DNA. He loved cooking and was often found in the kitchen at Calvert Street laboring over pots of marinara or steaming cauldrons of fresh linguine. Jake seemed to tick every stereotype box for a mobster ever represented in books and films.

***

In chess, regarding the positioning of your pieces, solid strategy requires setting goals for long-term play, as opposed to tactics that are more move-to-move oriented. While tactics, particularly at Master level, often decide a game, effective positioning must account for the safety of the king, the overall positions of the pieces as they develop, the pawn structure and the control of key squares, not to mention controlling important blocks of squares. Uncle Jake controlled the board—in his case, the neighborhood—like a true chess Master.

When the town filled with conventions of doctors or lawyers, Uncle Jake's crew would rent a suite of rooms at the Mount Royal Hotel or Belvedere Hotel. Those types of guys, that is, professionals, were easy marks because they lived and operated in a world of rules, taking people at their words. Jake exploited this—as he saw it—childish naiveté. They were now in his world. If they fell for his machinations, then it was on them, not him. He was strictly a businessman, and his business was operating outside the system these men understood.

Jake's people hired call girls to act as hospitality hostesses, with an improvised hotel room bar, along with a "friendly" card or dice game. The pigeons would come to roost and get fleeced after drinking too much, getting laid, then feeling dangerously comfortable to play games that were designed to vacuum the cash from their fat wallets.

For Uncle Jake's crew, fixing dice games was both an art and a science. They managed to sniff out which country clubs were having big parties, where and when the union halls would be packed with meetings or stake out the target-rich environment of easy marks in the black neighborhoods. The last two were potentially lethal as you did not want to get caught cheating at dice by either steelworkers or blacks, who often settled beefs with violence.

But Jake's men packed heat and were fearless, even entering other people's games they knew were fixed only to introduce *their own* loaded dice. The crew had a huge assortment of crooked dice that would match any other dice, crooked or not. After matching the other crew's fixed dice, they'd switch them out during the game and take control of the game before the other hustlers knew what hit 'em.

Cheating at dice can be a very tricky proposition. Loaded dice are clearly the best way to insure your numbers come up with consistency. However, if you're playing against anyone seasoned, it's sometimes hard to introduce your own pair of dice. Palming can work if the throw is short, but more savvy players require a wall bounce which negates that advantage.

A very experienced dice man can hold the dice a certain way, favoring the final position of the dice he wants to appear before they leave his hand and then throw them in a way that preserves the starting position in his hand. This technique usually requires a dice player to use a form of obfuscation like a magician would use, in this case snappy and distracting verbal banter and hand movements that give the appearance of a good roll but do not really affect the final positions of the dice after leaving the hand. This technique is hard to do and takes a great deal of practice. It also runs the risk of being divined by players who've seen it in operation. When they suspect this ploy, and particularly when you've had enough rolls to favor you (and especially when the other guy or guys have lost enough money), things can get ugly fast. Again, see the above for who *not* to be in the company of when this chicanery is sussed out.

But there were lots more ways Jake's guys made money using sleazy techniques.

As far as pure scams, and, yes, it was the mischief of sleazeballs, their wire-service con was a work of genius. First, they would prime their mark, often some bookie in a blue-collar neighborhood, over the course of maybe a week. One of the keys to this swindle was finding a bookie who was a regular Joe and none too bright. You didn't want a guy who had more common sense than greed. Or a suspicious mind.

Dressing up like working-class guys, Uncle Jake's crew would pick a member who they would send in regularly every day to place his bets and get to know the bookie...or, rather, him to know them. But each day he would lay his bets closer and closer to the post-time at the big tracks like Hialeah, Pimlico, Santa Anita and Aqueduct. Each day, they would hit or miss the bet. However, each day their "undercover agent" would up his bets so the bookie began to expect a pattern. Finally, at the end of the week, he would come in and lay down a huge bet to "try and win back the week's losses." Amazingly, he'd win. *Every time.*

How?

Remember, this was well before modern communications and instantaneous media. The second the race was over Jake and his guys had someone phone them with the results, and they'd immediately bet the winner with a huge wad moments before the bookie would find out the race was actually over. Seconds counted like minutes in this scam. Sometimes, as a distraction, they'd start a fight in the bar just before post-time to keep the bookie from reasoning through what was about to go down.

Another scam they played was the "Mr. Penn" or "Mr. Bell" score, as they called it. This, like almost all of their schemes, played upon the greed of their mark, usually a well-to-do businessman. They would figure out which chump was laying big bets with their own regular bookie. Then they'd call the mark, introduce themselves as Mr. Penn and ask for a favor. They would tell him his regular bookie was having a hard time handling the big shooter's wagers so "Mr. Penn," a new, higher rolling bookie had been asked to cover some of the big spender's action—sort of spreading the risk.

To take the bets, the "new bookie," either Jake or one of his guys, told their mark they'd be sending "Vincent" over (played by my stepfather, Ralph) to pick up the cash. If the guy won, they paid. If he lost, they collected. Just like normal. This would go on for maybe a month until the guy got comfortable with the new arrangement, and the hook was firmly in his mouth.

Then, they'd introduce a new wrinkle.

Ralph would offer a choice opportunity. The story would go that the cousin of the guy's regular bookie was "in trouble" and could rig it so the guy won every time, as long as the guy kicked back a little taste of the winnings, which was a sure thing. The mark loved this offer of a no-lose deal and would happily go along and win repeatedly, but after a while he'd get greedy (guaranteed!). Instead of a few thousand here and there, he'd ask to lay down maybe $30,000 or $40,000—a ton of money back when a new Caddie was five Gs.

This was the move Ralph had been awaiting. Ralph would tell the guy that, since it was such a big bet, he needed the cash up front, which the greedy sucker was all too willing to do, given he'd been doing quite well with Mr. Penn the hotshot bookie. Sadly, for the mark though, once the big bet was down, with the cash safely in Ralph's hands, Ralph would go *phfft*...into the wind, never to be seen again.

Usually, they ran that scam out of town, so the angry mark couldn't hunt them down, but sometimes they too would get greedy and pull it in their own backyard at the risk of getting seen and caught or worse. But true professionals that they were they actually had another scam in their pocket to get around that. If they took a local to the cleaners and feared being found out, Ralph would call the guy up and warn him that although they lost big, that was the least of "their" worries. Sounding as "injured" as he could, he'd take the guy into his confidence, informing him he was laid up in the hospital with numerous broken limbs and a broken back, payback for the scam against the bookie.

If the guy were a skeptic (as they often were after losing that kind of cake) and wanted to see for himself and went to Johns Hopkins, Ralph would actually be in a room, looking thoroughly wrecked in a cast from head to toe. It was as simple as Ralph knowing a doctor who would give him the room and get him rigged up in the cast (which came right off). Now the mark was scared so shitless of having his own legs, arms and back snapped he'd jackrabbit and gladly kiss the loss goodbye, having gotten out alive and with his bones intact. Jake and his crew called this stunt "the blow off." Brilliant.

Now that Jake was established as small-time gangster, he decided it was a good time to "settle" down. One night at The Band Box, a local swing joint where famous musicians like Tommy Dorsey, Frank Sinatra, Perry Como, Tony Bennett and Dean Martin would drop by, either to make the scene or perform or both, Jake met a striking redhead slinging cocktails named Peggy. A down-home country girl from North Carolina, Peggy was no dummy and figured out pretty fast what Jake did for a living. He was the opportunity she was looking to find, so she glommed onto him faster than you could say "Two Manhattan's, honey." Despite this knowledge (or perhaps because of it), she wasn't scared off and the two soon got married and moved into Calvert Street.

CHAPTER FOUR

King's Pawns

"The passed pawn is a criminal, who should be kept under lock and key.
Mild measures, such as police surveillance, are not sufficient."

—Aron Nimzowitsch, Chess Grandmaster

As I've described them, the pawns are the least important players on the board. However, they can come in handy and not just in getting across the board to become queens. The pawns are also very helpful in running interference against opposing players, and they are particularly useful to the king, especially when he castles behind a row of sacrificial pieces. The king enjoys his relative safety because he knows that whoever can get close to him has to take a pawn first, giving him a chance to use his single move in any direction to either escape or exact revenge.

The passed pawn, as Nimzowitsch observes, is quite dangerous as it can reach the eighth row and suddenly become a major threat and power center. The king (or queen) who regulates their game must keep an eye on passing pawns lest they achieve this level of sway and begin to feel they are the power center. Of course, in chess, the pieces are merely carved or molded from some inanimate material but, in real life, such "passing" pawns must be watched carefully. Most don't need extra concern since play—or life— tends to take them out of contention. Some pawns last the full game but usually do so by staying away from the worst conflict. Uncle Jake had many pawns around Calvert Street, many of them women. While he felt that women certainly had a place in his world, it was without a doubt subservient to him. Aunt Peggy learned to go with the flow.

***

Despite not being particularly tall at around five-five, Aunt Peggy stood out in a crowd because of her long, flowing red locks and large, firm bust. Peggy also had these gorgeous, sympathetic blue eyes that always seemed to tell you they cared. She generated this confidence in her that you could tell her your troubles and she'd actually listen.

Uncle Jake, on the other hand, was coarse looking, by all opinions a relatively unattractive man with a huge, round head and appropriately prominent ears, with a bulbous, misshapen nose. As I've mentioned, he glossed his ink-black hair with hair oil and combed it straight back to make it look more like a shiny appliance than hair. The one positive going for Jake's looks was his ability to pass as any of several ethnic backgrounds, a very valuable trait for hustling. Jake was slightly chunky but had been so since his youth and had grown to see it as one of his trademarks. His heft made him that much more intimidating for those who might challenge him. Aiding him in maintaining this size advantage was the fact that, at that time, men's fashions were baggy and loose-fitting. Wearing your beltline half-way up your chest and above your fat gut was not only okay, it was the style. Like any respectable hoodlum, Jake always sported the finest suits.

Aunt Peggy had only been in Baltimore two months when Jake met her at the Band Box. She was from Goldsboro, North Carolina. Only twenty-two-years old to Jake's thirty-six, she had a soft Southern accent that added to her feminine gentleness. A great sadness of her life was leaving behind a daughter fathered by a one-night stand. Jake had earned points with Peggy by offering to get the child and raise her as his own. But the decision was made to leave her in North Carolina, because the girl by then believed that someone else was her mother and no one wanted to further complicate the child's life. Jake was enchanted by Peggy and gave her the respect he'd withheld from the poor, hapless human-trafficked Mary. But he was older and more mature, if not necessarily more compassionate. Jake by then understood a little more about using people through charm, as opposed to simply forcing them into brutal subservience.

It didn't take long for Peggy to succumb to his charisma, not to mention the power she perceived he had, and she soon moved in and quickly adapted to the grifter's lifestyle. It would only be a matter of weeks before Jake would enlist her in one of his pet scams.

"Peggy," he announced grandly, "I'm going to let you in on this next job."

"Really?" responded Peggy, eager to be trusted. "How can I help?"

"Well Peg, I found a barber named Joe who is takin' book up on Belair Road so I started gettin' all my shaves and haircuts by him, all the while pickin' his brain, asking questions about any action he might be in on or heard about. So, after the fourth shave, he comes out and says he don't take no book, but Fat Martha his wife does. Can you imagine a dame takin' book? Well, I figured I hit some pay dirt—I knew he was holdin' out. Anyhow, so Joe trusts me and gives me her phone number. I ask him how's she doin', and he says, *'Hey, she's fat and old, how's she supposed to be doin'?'* So's I call her up, and when she gets on the phone, I talk real sweet to her, like, 'This is Jake, can I speak to Martha?' 'Yeah,' she says, 'this is me, who's this?' 'Wow sweetie,' I says, 'what a sweet voice,' and she says, 'I never heard that one before, asshole, now what are you betting on?' I'm tellin' ya, I had to laugh!"

Jake gave her the name of a horse that was sure to lose. How did he know that? Because the jockey, Billy, who was riding him was holding the horse back...for Jake. So, Jake would continually lose races where Billy rode, and then he'd pay off at Joe's the Barber. He'd call again and again, playing sure losers for small stakes, all the while sweet-talking Martha.

Jake waited until the time was right and made his move. He asked to meet Martha. She gave Jake the address, and it wasn't too long before he'd sweet-talked his way into her bed. While Jake wasn't exactly Douglas Fairbanks, Jr., Martha wasn't exactly Maureen O'Hara. Truth was Martha hadn't been fucked in years. Soon after Jake began dipping his prosciutto in her marinara, she was sweet on Jake. Ever the gentleman, he strategically leaves that aspect of the story out of his version to Peggy.

Jake then explains to Peggy, "Martha lives off 25th Street, and there's an alley outside the kitchen window. Go find a dog, I don't care where or how, but make sure you walk the dog in the alley."

On that day, Jake insists he'll make spaghetti for lunch for Martha. Perpetually hungry, Martha is happy, knowing Jake is a pretty good cook, and this is one of his signature dishes. Positioned at a phone booth on the corner of 25th and Barclay was one of his guys, Dough-Dough. The race goes off at Pimlico at exactly one o'clock. The race finishes at one-oh-three, and Dough Dough holds up three fingers to Peggy, signaling the three horse had won.

Peggy quickly makes for the alley and holds up three fingers to Jake in the kitchen window where he's cooking his spaghetti and waiting for her high-sign. After getting the intel from Peggy, Jake carries two full, steaming plates of spaghetti into the living room where four phones were constantly ringing.

"Here you go, lovey, both plates are for you!" Jake told her.

Fat Martha's capacious keister was overtaxing the poor little swivel stool in front of the dining room table, a phone in each ear. On the cluttered table were dozens of paper betting slips and an ashtray choked with butts, two or three cigarettes still smoldering. Jake eyed the pile of debris to find a landing place for the plates. Meanwhile, Martha was distracted from handling call after call, like a Ma Bell switchboard operator on Mother's Day.

"Seventh horse, fourth race Pimlico, two hundred to win. You're down Mickey."

"Exacta box six and three, fifth race Pimlico, eighty bucks. You're down Al."

"Put the plates down right there, hon," said Fat Martha, indicating a relatively bare spot at the corner of the table, a smoke hanging from the corner of her pie hole.

Jake shoved the detritus aside and laid the plates down, then, almost as an afterthought, smooth as butter sank the knife into her.

"Oh, yeah, I almost forgot, love, here's my bet."

He handed her a tight green roll of thirty portraits of America's first Postmaster General. Three Gs, cold.

"Big spender!" she said, grabbing the roll. "What horse and what race? You know you've never placed a winner with me yet."

"Put it all on the number three horse, first race at Pimlico. I feel lucky."

Fat Martha glanced at her watch. It was 1:08 and the race went off at 1:00 but Jake had been in the kitchen making spaghetti and had no access to a phone.

"You're down, hon."

And with that Martha took the bet...and the hook, square in the mouth of one of the best sucker scams Jake ever contrived.

The horse paid $14 for a two-dollar bet. Of course, Jake didn't bet two bucks, he bet three thousand which netted him $21,000. Sometimes, the biggest scores were as simple as having access to a wire service, a phone booth, three fingers and the ability to cook up a killer marinara.

Jake also knew he'd found a one-of-a-kind woman in Peggy: a perfect mate and a partner in crime. Even though Jake didn't tell her, Peggy knew through the grapevine he was fucking that cow, but she didn't bat an eyelash. She knew for a good score sometimes personal feelings had to be put aside. Twenty-one-thousand clams back then bought you a very decent house in the suburbs. Peggy understood the concept of the price of doing business. In that respect, Peggy was a diehard pragmatist.

Uncle Jake loved running his scams at or near the track but eventually had to limit his criminal activities to outside the track because he'd been banned for fixing races among many other infractions that finally had the track management just put an end to Mr. Frederick Juliano's hijinks and eighty-six him. This cramped his style, but he just set up camp at a bar near Pimlico to break down his Racing Form every day.

Jake was quite good at calculating the odds using a variety of factors, just as an orbital analyst for NASA could calculate the trajectory of a spacecraft's reentry into the atmosphere. Jake would work the form, then use those results to dispatch his cadre of touts and scammers to use the information to their—and his—advantage. Jake was like the hub of a wheel of deceit and his spokes kept that wheel spinning. Jake was damn good at picking the winners—more often than not—but when he'd hit the occasional bad streak, he'd be hell to be around.

Jake populated his apartment building with show girls and street hookers along with bookies, touts and jockeys from Pimlico. He liked track people, and he liked working women, perhaps because they all seemed to be operating on the side of the law (that is, the *wrong side*) where Jake was comfortable.

Everyone got special perks because Jake had his fingers in everything they did, from the hooker's take from each john to the jockeys, bookies and touts who would fix races (see above) for their landlord. Uncle Jake and Aunt Peggy lived on the first floor, and their kitchen was his Oval Office, the central meeting place for the entire building, open day and night, giving Uncle Jake a chance to hold court and show off his cooking skills for an army of hangers-on, just like in his jailhouse days.

Right out of *Goodfellas* or *The Godfather*, Uncle Jake always had a huge pot of gravy—as the Italians called marinara sauce—on the stove. Anyone who entered the kitchen got fed, hungry or not. He was like a Jewish grandmother with muscle. You never said no to Uncle Jake, and as an Italian he refused to believe anyone could *not* be hungry. Uncle Jake would give you the shirt off his back or a place to stay.

But if it was *cash* you needed, "Fuhgeddaboutit!"

As a guy who smelled money as efficiently as a shark smells blood, no matter who you were or how broke or rich you were, Uncle Jake was always thinking of ways to take money off of you. But *give* you cash? No way. *No. Way.*

Uncle Jake had been quite the ladies' man in his younger days and, this lifestyle, particularly given his lack of discretion in choosing his partners, saw him contract syphilis and, as a result, it had rendered him sterile. Since Peggy and he couldn't have their own children, as time passed, they felt they were missing something in their perfect life. Then fate intervened when a trolley car hit and killed one of Uncle Jake's brothers. And out of that tragedy came a blessing. At least it seemed like that at the time. Uncle Jake's brother left a young widow and his son, nine-year-old Ralph.

Young Ralph would visit them on holidays, and Uncle Jake and Aunt Peggy soon developed an attachment for the fatherless kid. When his mother remarried a burly, abusive Pole who beat the crap out of little Ralph, he fled to Uncle Jake's and Aunt Peggy's. They took him in and began raising him as their own. Uncle Jake seized the opportunity and took Ralph under his wing, tutoring the boy in how to act and dress for success. Sharpness of thought, words and attire were Uncle Jake's hallmarks, and Ralph had the art of sharpness drilled into him 24/7. Ralph became a hustler prodigy under Uncle Jake's tutelage. This was the world into which Ralph brought my mother and me.

***

One of my first memories of Uncle Jake was that horrendous scar defacing nearly his entire right arm, the result of that injury and rum-running conviction that landed him in the pokey. Deep and cavernous, the hole in his flesh went nearly to the bone, like some fiendish land-born shark had nearly gotten the whole limb. I remember wondering how his arm could even work with that gaping void of muscle and tissue. He delighted in seeing my child eyes widen in horror as he described how the hospital had treated the wound with maggots, filling the savage maw in his body with the crawling whitish mass of pre-insects to devour the infected tissue. It was an obscene image to download into a child's psyche, but Jake seemed to delight in my expressions of disgust.

Perhaps to take away from the horror of his right arm, his left arm featured a real oddity: a tattoo of a lady with the body a penguin. I always wondered who conceived of such a grotesquerie, but it paled to the maggot image, and I was content to ogle the penguin girl. When he wasn't in one of his trademark suits, his arms were almost always visible as he wore a shirt common among working-class Italians back then, the infamous "wife beater" tank shirt worn by everyone from Mafia soldiers to Marlon Brando in *A Streetcar Named Desire*. To incongruously round out his attire, Uncle Jake would wear sharp and expensive dress slacks along with Italian shoes polished to magnificence like leather mirrors. He was simply a white dress shirt—with the now famous small-spread mob collar with long points, silk tie and perfectly pressed jacket—away from sartorial resplendence. Bruce Wayne in his cape, tights and utility belt, merely in need of his mask to be Batman.

CHAPTER FIVE

Controlling the Center

"The blunders are all there on the board, waiting to be made."

—Savielly Tartakower, Chess Grandmaster

The little boy sat in his high chair eating his breakfast of scrambled eggs. He was around two-and-a-half-years old. The kitchen was functional, small and working class for North Carolina. The older couple were nearby, the wife cleaning some dishes and the husband sipping coffee and reading the morning newspaper. It was a normal, quiet morning in this normal, quiet little town. Few things worked to rattle the lazy pace of life in the rural south in the late fifties.

As the little boy's tiny fork tapped against the compartmentalized melamine plate, scooping up the last tasty tidbits of egg, the back door burst open and a man entered, breathing hard, eyes bugged, a revolver in his hand. The man sitting at the table nearby leapt up in terror. His wife, drying a plate, let it crash to the floor.

"Get back!" screamed the crazed gunman. They complied. The little boy, upset by the wild man bursting into their calm kitchen, began to cry. The gunman suddenly snatched the little boy from his highchair, keeping his gun leveled at the couple so that they would not resist. Then he bolted out the door. Soon the gunman and the little boy were on a bus heading north to Baltimore.

The kidnapping and bus ride were the little boy's first memories.

On the bus, the gunman gave the little boy a toy, a little man with a huge head seated in a yellow car. The little man's huge head kept falling off, much to the child's dismay.

The crazed gunman and little boy made it to Baltimore in two days.

The gunman was a small-time hood with dreams of being a made man in the Mafia. His name was Ralph Juliano, my stepfather.

I was the little boy.

***

Controlling the center four squares of a chessboard is so important the lesson is drilled into the head of every young chess player. Holding dominion over those four pieces of real estate is essential to winning any game. They are the Northwest Passage, the Panama Canal, the Strait of Gibraltar, the Silk Road of your game. By having your pieces in such positions that you hold sway over that center area, you increase your chances of winning by a large degree.

His home at 1315 North Calvert was Uncle Jake's board center, his four squares. It was chosen to give him and his minions access to moneymaking schemes but was also convenient for hiding out or working from that centralized location. North Calvert was the Mecca to his religion of grift. Jake was no dummy and, over the years in his hard-won victories on the street, he'd learned that a home base had to have certain qualities to effectively support a number of scams. And, with Calvert, he had chosen the location with the precision and tactical foresight of a diamond cutter sizing up a rare stone.

After Ralph had sent my mother back from California and she was settled in Baltimore, she had been very anxious to get me back, perhaps because she was now four months pregnant with Ralph's child and her maternal instinct was stirring again. Meanwhile, my new "mother," Shirley, along with her husband, had since relocated to Greensboro, North Carolina. Barely back from their more than a year on the road (after promising Shirley it would only be "a few weeks"), my mother rushed down to Greensboro to retrieve me, but Shirley wasn't quite so willing to let go of the little boy she'd grown to love like her own...and feel as if he was her own.

She hid me from my mother and refused to hand me over, citing (probably legitimately) concerns about Georgia's vagabond and seemingly irresponsible lifestyle. My mother wanted her son back but was terrified to phone the FBI because she was now in deep with a pack of professional criminals and fringe people. Ralph got wind of this reluctance on Shirley's part to do the right thing and managed to sober up enough to return from California. When he got back, infuriated over the "kidnapping," Ralph's hot head hatched a plan and, like the true mobster he aspired to be, off he went to Greensboro, gat in hand.

The enraged Ralph stormed down to North Carolina by bus (being Cadillac-less) and, assuming negotiations were a fool's errand with Shirley and her husband, repo-ed me at gunpoint. Shirley cried hysterically when I was taken away. Say what you will about his methods, they did work, and, after the long bus ride, my mother and I were reunited.

While Ralph's "heroic" ride to bust me out seemed slightly chivalrous, his treatment of my mother was at best contemptible. As I mentioned, during her pregnancy Ralph began to distance himself from her because he found her growing belly unattractive. He took every opportunity to let her know she'd lost her appeal to him, and it hurt her deeply, not just over the alienation aspect, but for the chilling idea in the back of her mind that since she was carrying the man's child it would bind her to him forever.

But that concern was allayed one day when she experienced pains and was admitted to the hospital. The result? She lost the baby to a miscarriage. Now she wouldn't necessarily have to worry about the long-term connection to Ralph, but she was crushed nevertheless. Ralph, being the concerned and loving man, went to the hospital and confronted my mother in bed over money.

Prior to her going into the hospital, and after Ralph had made a rare good score, she pleaded with him to give her some money to open a bank account with which to pay bills and buy food for when he was absent on gambling runs. She firmly insisted that leaving her with no money and no contact number was no way to run a railroad. He grudgingly handed over $800 with which my mother immediately opened an account.

But now Ralph was in her room at the hospital raising a ruckus because he'd gone into a hole again and need cash to get himself out. He screamed at her to leave the hospital, go to the bank and get him "the goddamned money!" When she finally got released from the hospital, rather than be there to pick her up and comfort her, Ralph instead went and parked himself on the front rail of a titty-bar, handing out tips to the dancers and drinking his cash away.

***

Our home at 1315 North Calvert was a veritable rogue's gallery of colorful people. When you watch a movie about Mafia guys, know that their nicknames are usually no exaggeration because fanciful nicknames are an old Italian tradition. Jake's crew consisted of a number of tough and eccentric characters, including the aforementioned Dough-Dough, a corpulent Italian who operated as Jake's main muscle. There was the aptly-named Charlie Bananas because, obviously, he was...well... crazy. Another Charlie, Charlie Cammarada, was a short, slight man with beady doll-like eyes whose idiosyncratic affectation was to carry his Chihuahua everywhere. He was lucky not to get the mob handle Charlie Chihuahua.

Johnny was a retired boxer who married the sister of famous ecdysiast Blaze Starr, a personal friend of Aunt Peggy. Johnny would often keep his boxing skills sharp by beating her, and one time we watched the poor woman climbing up a tree in front of the apartment house to escape another beating. When Johnny hit pay dirt with a major score, he bought a used car lot and instituted a business model of preying on mostly impoverished African Americans with ridiculous interest rates. A kind, sensitive man, Johnny would troll through the streets of a black neighborhood, Cherry Hill, in a tow truck with chains jangling behind to let everyone know that repossession was but one missed payment away.

Another member of the Calvert asylum was Henri, a broken-down former jockey who joined Uncle Jake in being banned from Pimlico for race fixing. Also, like Jake, Henri had a bad limp, this one not from running from the cops but rather from being thrown from a horse. Henri, like many of the miscreants living with us, did not have a dime to his name. But that didn't preclude big ambitions: Henri clung to this dream of one day blackmailing J. Edgar Hoover. This animus stemmed from a claim he made of seeing Hoover years before, participating in a sex act at the Mayflower Hotel in D.C. It seemed odd the man begrudged the former G-Man a little extracurricular fun, but, given Mr. Hoover's proclivities, it could have been Henri's inability to countenance non-heterosexual pleasure. Or, given that he was one of the Calvert Street crew, he may have just had a wildly active imagination. Read: hallucinations.

Whenever Henri could get away with it, he would park himself at Uncle Jake's phone to try and reach Hoover. It appears he may have had all the details of the blackmail sorted out, from the introduction of his damning evidence to the mechanics of collecting the hush money. Once or twice, he actually got through and, apparently, during his presentation with either Hoover himself or a subordinate, Henri threatened to spill the beans on the down-low hanky panky if John Edgar didn't pony up some sweet dough-re-mi. The blackmail money never materialized but soon after the FBI did arrive to escort Henri away. With his phone call, he sort of uniquely redefined suicide by cop.

***

Uncle Jake was a racist. As in a RACIST. Uncle Jake never seemed to refer to anyone's ethnicity, nationality or religion in normal, civilized terms. No, Italians were dagos, Jews were kikes or Hebes, Poles were Polacks, and blacks were niggers. While the fifties and sixties represented a great struggle by many for equality and human rights, Jake merely saw it all as a stunt, and they just missed the point that he, a white man (never mind that he was 100% Italian heritage), was superior. End of discussion. Women were included in that hierarchy of inferiority, but he had slightly warmer feeling toward the fairer sex so his antipathy towards them was slightly better concealed. It was just the way it was back then. And with him.

Uncle Jake saw a young black boy playing in the alley one day, so he put him to work, painting and cleaning for pocket money. The boy's name was James, but to Uncle Jake he was always called Nigger James. Believe me, Uncle Jake was no Mark Twain, and this was around 1960, not 1860. As the years went by, James could always rely on Uncle Jake to give him work to do for a wage, meals, clothes, shoes and a place to stay on the open back porch facing the alley.

I remember James sleeping on the wooden porch in the sweltering Baltimore summer. I would sit with him as a young boy, and I asked him why Uncle Jake called him Nigger James.

He seemed puzzled and shrugged at my ignorance. "'Cause I'm a nigger."

He was wholly unaware that men and women named Martin Luther King, Rosa Parks, Malcom X and countless others were at that very moment fighting for James right to never be called that word.

James was also a hustler. He was a good-looking young man whose eye whites (the sclera) were always a jaundiced yellow. I don't think he was by any means alone in this quality, and I can find no medical condition to indicate there was anything wrong with him. In other words, it's kind of common, particularly among American blacks as well as Africans. James was also quite the player and had six or seven girlfriends going at any given time, with a habit of collecting welfare money from each of them at the first of every month. I'm still not sure why he col-lected the money (he wasn't a pimp) but he seemed to take quite seri-ously the process of collection. One month, one of the women would not give him money. In a fit of rage, he killed her. James was caught hiding at Uncle Jake's and given a life sentence, and that was the end of his tenure at Calvert, and, I presume, anywhere but a concrete box.

Everyone in Uncle Jake's universe knew that he was the boss. No one argued with him. No one contradicted him, no one called him on much of anything. That is, except my mother. Almost from the time Ralph moved us all into 1315 North Calvert, my mother and Jake began having words. It all came about when Jake began to realize that Ralph's young wife, Georgia, seemed to see through his bluster and didn't appear to fear him like everyone else. Like everyone else *was sup-posed to fear him.*

My mother saw Jake as a fat drunken bully. And, when it came down to it, a coward. Yes, he seemed to have his fingers in a lot of pots, some legitimate like a nightclub and a car lot, but he was ultimately a guy who lived on the edge of the law, and she didn't take him that seri-ously. This lack of deference came probably because she had a yardstick of her own with which to judge men who lived to an extreme code: her own father Ed who, truth be told, might have eaten Uncle Jake for breakfast and still been hungry. More on him soon.

She also wasn't particularly impressed by the crowd that populated North Calvert. She knew Jake was a hoodlum, but she sized him up as being a smaller, more two-bit grifter than he wanted anyone to see him. He wanted to be Lucky Luciano and, while most of the local rubes saw him that way, my mother didn't. She felt that Jake was more of a lucky-to-have-what-he's-got nickel-and-dime bamboozler.

Despite the scams and grifts and people paying homage to Jake and the hidden panels throughout 1315 North Calvert stocking cash, guns and other booty, she saw the collection of human driftwood as the dregs and their leader a pompous blowhard. She also saw a lot of Jake in Ralph and that might have bothered her the most. She knew that Ralph was in

Jake's sway and had been so since he was a child, and she resented Ralph for his childish adoration of a chunky middle-aged man she saw simply as a lucky punk.

She also was concerned that Ralph had changed a lot, even since they'd been on the road where he exposed himself as an erratic, hot-headed lush. But at least he'd seemed to love her. Or perhaps lust after her. But now that she was pregnant again—and worse, in Ralph's opinion—*showing*, he seemed to turn on her. He upped his drinking and abuse toward her and mocked her shape, complaining that she wasn't the hot young thing he'd married.

Well, yeah...*she was pregnant.*

Also, like a true odds maker, he set her up for a pretty good chance of failure by telling everyone she was going to have a boy and *he only wanted a boy.* The fifty/fifty odds of failure weighed on my mother as she carried the baby. My mother also began to look around at the others living with her and make judgments.

She saw Aunt Peggy in a more sympathetic light but felt Peggy was a woman wasting her life. Peggy was clearly a woman under stress as she eventually settled into a pattern of being hammered on pills most of the time. While Jake's weakness was alcohol, Peggy usually ingested the powerful opioid Percocet but would take any sedative she could get. She had a list of doctors who were happy to prescribe her pills. She'd be in a perpetually altered state, primarily to block out the pain of Uncle Jake's serial fucking around with the showgirls lodging in the building. If, in a moment of weakness, she complained or got out of line, Jake would beat the crap out of her. Thus, Peggy took the path of least resistance and that was a whole lot easier in a drugged-out state of who-gives-a-shit.

Another resident of the building was Cora Lee, an ex-stripper and Peggy's friend. They would get high on pills together. In a state of pill-enhanced beatitude, Aunt Peggy and Cora Lee would walk around the apartment building wearing robes with nothing on underneath. As a child, I felt a new and exciting sensation when their robes fluttered open by accident. Too young to understand the emotions it created, I would sometimes lie on the floor and pretend to play with my toy soldiers just to get a glimpse up their robes at their naked bodies.

My sister Marie was born when I was three. Unlike pretty much everyone else in his life, Ralph was actually crazy about her, despite his betting against a girl. But Ralph couldn't keep his dick in his pants. When my mother caught him fucking Cora Lee, the feces hit the spinning metal wind generator. This was the first time I remember her packing up my sister and me and heading to Savannah in the middle of the night while everyone was asleep.

CHAPTER SIX

The Rook

"Find what you love and let it kill you."
—Charles Bukowski

Historically, chess sees the rook as a power piece. Stronger than the bishop or knight, the rook often symbolized the machinery of war. In medieval shatranj, the rook represented a chariot. To the Persians who took it a step further, the rook was a heavily-armored chariot, more of a weapons system back then, scythes bristling from the wheels and replete with a driver and bowman, ready to launch his quiver full of arrows into the opposing soldiers. The rook has always been the king's Lancelot, ready to defend him, even to lay down his life for his liege. The rook is tough, uncompromising, perhaps even dogmatic, its moves limited strictly to vertical and horizontal, forward and backward only, but taking as many spaces as it wants to move—unless it gets to jump that one time—but only in service to his king. In the end, the rook is a serious man, a man not to be fucked with.

A man like Ed Noonan.

***

Over the next five years, I couldn't begin to recall how many times my mother left Ralph. She would leave because of his countless infidelities with everyone, from Jake's hookers to drug addicts and the other bottom feeders who surrounded us. Sometimes Ralph would go on month-long drinking binges or instigate horrific fights that made *Who's Afraid of Virginia Wolfe* look like a Soupy Sales sketch.

Ralph was also a bit of an amateur magician in that he could take money, in any amount or denomination, and make it disappear. He would make a score and rather than salt some of it away he'd shoot over to Atlantic City and—poof!—it would be gone. This cycle began to wear on my mother, along with the conveyor belt of sleazy women to whom Ralph would attach himself. In that respect, he was just like Jake, and my mother had long since seen the parallels and written them both off as losers, despite Jake's apparent success.

To my mother, despite Jake's outward show of providing for those around him, deep down Jake worried about Jake and no one else. If he seemed concerned about you, it was because he wanted something from you. She saw him as a failure as a man. But one thing my mother admitted about Jake: he always treated my sister and me well. But Jake's outsized cynicism and Ralph's learned sociopathy—coupled with their excesses with the bottle—simply wore her out, and she would reach a breaking point, exacerbated by some event—what, it didn't matter as they were all of a piece—and we'd find ourselves fleeing South.

***

Our haven away from Ralph and the chaos of Calvert was in Savannah, Georgia, at the home of my mother's parents. Carol and Ed Noonan (a.k.a. Grandma and Granddaddy Noonan) lived on Richardson Creek near Tybee Island, maybe ten miles from the outskirts of Savannah. Tybee Island has the dubious distinction of being the only American soil where Americans dropped a hydrogen bomb.

Yes, we dropped an H-bomb on ourselves.

On February 5, 1958, two Air Force aircraft, an F-86 fighter jet and a B-47 bomber, collided during an exercise. The bomber was carrying a 7,600-pound Mark 15 thermonuclear bomb. The F-86 was no longer airworthy so the pilot punched out and survived. The bomber, on the other hand, dropped considerably in altitude, but the pilot was able to regain control. To maintain their control over the stricken craft, the crew asked permission to jettison their very heavy payload, the thermonuclear device in their bomb bay. They were also worried (understandably) that the bomb might just go off were they to crash land. They got the go-ahead to unload it and at 7200 feet...bombs away! The official word at the time was that the bomb was not a fully functional weapon, having had the nuclear trigger and plutonium core removed. But in a 1966 Congressional hearing, an assistant Secretary of Defense testified that the unit was a fully functional device, "a complete weapon, a bomb with a nuclear capsule." Had the bomb detonated, experts say that pretty much everything would have been incinerated within a radius of 1.2 miles at a temperature of over ten thousand degrees. Fortunately, the bomb didn't detonate, but it deeply embarrassed the U.S. military as it should have. And less comforting, it was merely one off many, many accidents the military has had with its nuclear toys.

Richardson Creek was more river than creek with extensive marsh land beyond the mudflats on low tide. I learned to swim in that river. With me tied to a rope, Granddaddy would throw me off one side of the dock and the current would take me down river. He would reel me in and land me back on the dock to start it all over again. One of thirteen children, Granddaddy Noonan's impressively productive mother was a full Cherokee Indian. The story went that his father made her his bride after serving in the U.S. Cavalry. Georgia was a real melting pot of American Indian tribes, and they had a proud history of habitation of the area going back before 10,000 B.C.

Despite only a sixth-grade education, Granddaddy Noonan was a sort of self-taught Ben Franklin and Henry Ford rolled into one when it came to all things mechanical, learning everything he could on his own about machinery. By the time he was an adult, he was a master of diesel mechanics, internal combustion, rotary engines and steam power, with some rocket technology and theory thrown in for good measure.

As I mentioned earlier, he also had a fascination with the products of Volkswagenwerk AG and became quite adept at fixing them. He admired their clever engineering and simplicity. As a master mechanic, he could pretty much fix anything with moving parts, and he got a job with the Southern Paper Board Company making sure their miles of machinery and mechanical systems were always working properly.

As a U.S. Marine, Granddaddy Noonan had fought in Okinawa during World War II. U.S. soldiers called Okinawa the "Typhoon of Steel," while Japanese soldiers similarly referred to it as *tetsu no ame*, or "Rain of Steel," to describe the horrors of that pivotal and extended battle. By all accounts, Grandaddy Noonan was never the same after the war. Back then they called it "shell-shocked," but now we call it PTSD, an acronym for post-traumatic stress disorder. Being under fire for such an extended period of time with death sitting on your shoulder, ready to spirit you away at any given second, would drive even the sanest man not so sane.

It didn't help matters that Ed Noonan was also bipolar.

Here's a story that tends to graphically illustrate the type of man Granddaddy Ed Noonan was. Even as a young man, Ed understood his own power, physically and intellectually. He tended to naturally dominate everyone around him, women or men.

At boot camp, a husky hillbilly from Tennessee had couched a dislike for a certain thin Italian city boy in the unit, for what reason no one knew, but every morning he decided it would be fun to terrorize the kid by throwing a Bowie knife into the wood of his bunk, a mere half-inch from the boy's head. Despite being a real boor, the hillbilly was astonishingly adept at tossing his knife.

Ed, who only stood as high as the bully's chest, decided one day he'd had enough of the campaign to serially humiliate the city kid and just came out and told the perpetrator, "Don't do it again." His voice was firm but unemotional. The bully mistook Ed's quiet resolve for a lack of commitment and turned on him.

Disbelieving this sawed-off little runt was giving him orders, the looming hillbilly sized up Ed as his next victim. He pushed back verbally but moved closer to his smaller adversary. The argument heated to the point the hillbilly got angry enough to finally throw a punch straight at Ed's face. What happened next had many of those GIs telling the story the rest of their lives, as if they'd witnessed Achilles besting Hector.

Ed Noonan calmly caught the punch in midair, as if it was a baseball casually tossed to him. He then applied pressure to the sad sack's fist, as if it were in a vise. Even as a young man, his years of constantly twisting wrenches gave Ed forearms like Popeye and a grip to rival an anaconda. He practically crushed the bones in the man's hand until the sniveling coward fell to his knees and pleaded for his hand back with the promise never to throw the knife again. This epitomized how Ed Noonan handled problems. Extremes of strength and resolve of a type most men were not familiar.

***

Granddaddy Ed Noonan made sure that my mother's three younger brothers joined the Navy or Army, never the Marines, when they eventually had to join the service. Granddaddy Noonan had these huge brown eyes that were almost bulging like the late British actor/comedian Marty Feldman's (a sufferer of Graves' disease), but he was still oddly handsome. A stocky, powerful man, he enjoyed fighting, probably due to the combination of bipolar and PTSD. Granddaddy Noonan was a hair-triggered, dangerous individual.

To make things even less stable, he always carried a gun. Only slightly less deadly, he also possessed an arsenal of jokes second to none and never missed an opportunity to trot them out. Once, he and some friends went hunting in the Carolina back country and got caught in a torrential rainstorm lasting almost eighteen hours. For five of those hours, Granddaddy entertained his friends with joke after joke, going by category, beginning with dog jokes, then cheating wife jokes and slowly unrolling his repertoire of black, white, Polish, Jewish, hillbilly and any other category you could imagine. Had he been there, even fellow bigot Uncle Jake likely would have laughed. Bob Hope had a team of writers for the sheer volume of jokes that Granddaddy Noonan was able to command from memory. When the storm passed, the hunter's jaws were numb, never having laughed so hard in their lives.

A seemingly endless river of freight cars flowed steadily through the valley, delivering logs to the Southern Paper Board Company, located at the nexus of a huge web of tracks.

Day and night, a queue of cars lined up beside the giant roller belts, six-feet-wide and sixty-feet-long. The huge logs would roll off and glide gracefully into the chipper machines and grinders to be masticated into a usable size. The chips and bark were then poured into massive pump systems that acted as great digesters, forming what is called a slurry mix of fiber and acids that would break down into a pulp and get blown out onto large wire screens. Wet felt belts would press against the screens, picking up the paper and feeding it into the sets of drying rollers.

This was Ed Noonan's kingdom.

He was the master and commander of miles of machinery and mechanical systems that cried out for his expertise. There wasn't a gear, belt or control panel he didn't know intimately. Ed would spend his days in machine-driven bliss, attending to the constant breakdowns and problems, sometimes displaying an extraordinary inventiveness. Over the years, Ed had personally torn down and rebuilt all of the plant's machinery.

The plant would sometimes plan a "cold shut down" where operations would cease for ten long days while Ed and his team of mechanics worked eighteen-hour shifts overhauling the bearings and parts, scrutinizing every piece, cleaning, lubricating and adjusting to perfection. Before the plant could stop operating though, certain preparations needed to be made, and Ed would then add night shifts to his schedule for a number of days before the overhaul. Due to his odd and lengthy hours, he would sometimes need a nap to refresh himself, so he could keep going well into the night...or the next day.

Ed would find out-of-the-way places, such as the cage at the top of the elevator shaft, to lie down to catch some sleep. He'd time his naps for the factory whistle—three short blasts and one long one signaling breaks and shift changes—no matter where he was in the factory, as long as he could hear the whistle, his plan for solitude was secure, and he never even had to consult his watch, since the whistles blew like clockwork.

Here is another story that helps paint a picture of Ed Noonan and what you could expect from him in certain situations. This probably happened in the late fifties, more than a dozen years after Granddaddy had returned from the South Pacific.

My Uncle John, Mom's youngest brother, was in high school and got into a fight with a black student. They lit into each other pretty good, resulting in some black eyes and split lips, so John was hauled into the principal's office, and the principal told John he was going to make a phone call and get one of his parents to the school *immediately*.

Terrified how his folks, especially his father, might take this, John begged the principal not to call his home. He knew his mother was at the college taking classes and his father was asleep, having worked the night shift. He knew that if the phone woke his father it would be bad enough, but the nature of the phone call would cause Edward Noonan to declare a state of Defcon 1.

He was also painfully aware that his father was an old-school Southern man and many old-school Southern men were, shall we say, less than tolerant of civil rights and diversity, and he might not be so sanguine to discover his son's opponent in the brawl had been of color. John thought of the German Luger his father kept holstered to the sun visor in his Volkswagen bus. The gun he called his "nigger killer." And this disturbing piece of trivia tended to conflict with the fact, at face value at least, that Ed Noonan seemed to get along with black folks and even called a number of them his acquaintances. Not necessarily friends, but he knew them and was amiable with them. But actions spoke louder than bullshit small talk to Ed Noonan.

John shivered inside as the principal dialed the phone to make the fateful call.

He winced when, after quite a few rings, he heard someone answer and even across the room could hear the irritation in his father's voice. The principal sternly recounted John's list of sins in the fight with the black kid and sternly demanded, "You need to get down here right away because we're going to have a talk about your son."

John closed his eyes in fear at the principal's goading of his father. The man clearly had no idea who he was dealing with. John gulped when his father's response was terse and absolute. He was on his way.

John couldn't help what he said next but did so partly to protect the principal or foreshadow at least the approaching shit storm.

"You shouldn't have done that."

The principal dismissed the young man's admonition, taking it as his weak attempt to throw the guilt off himself and avoid his comeuppance. John was merely trying to warn the principal he was in for his own comeuppance.

John took a deep breath and just sat there waiting for the tornado. It came.

When Granddaddy Ed Noonan busted through the door, his face was livid, resembling a giant tomato. As the principal rose to say something, Granddaddy was removing his belt and forming it into a loop. Before the principal could react, Granddaddy had come around the desk, overpowered the man and thrown the leather belt around his neck and cinched it as efficiently as a Thuggee assassin. The principal struggled feebly as his face became a lovely shade of mottled purple. Ed Noonan's python grip pulled that belt tighter than Dick's hatband, and the principal's knees buckled.

"Lemme set you straight, mistah. Don't *ever* tell a Noonan what he's gotta do! You understand me, you pissant? I could fill one o' your classrooms up with the Japs I've killed!"

With that impressive claim, the principal passed out.

Ed's death gaze now moved to a wide-eyed John who gave a quick and accurate account of the fight in the hall.

Ed's eyes blazed as he listened, putting his belt back on.

He nodded and turned to go, his business complete. Well, almost, as he heard a moan from behind the desk as the principal regained his consciousness, if not his ability to swallow. Ed put both hands on the desk and leaned over it.

"Mistah, let another nigger touch my son, and I'll be at this god-damn school so fast it'll make Sherman's March look like a church social."

That was the Granddaddy Noonan Method of Conflict Resolution.

***

Carol Noonan, a.k.a. Grandma Noonan, was a half-Jewish girl from Brooklyn. Exceptionally smart (a prerequisite for keeping up with Granddaddy Noonan who was quite intelligent despite his often-primal responses to negative stimuli), she stood barely five-feet-tall and had this striking jet-black hair and brilliantly intense ebony eyes.

Carol, born in 1918, had been a timid child with a nervous condition, so to coax her out of her shell, her widowed mother (whom I knew as my Nana) enrolled her in dance classes at age four. After the dance instructor told Nana her child was gifted, Nana was soon dragging her around Manhattan for various auditions in the growth industry known as showbiz.

Young Carol quickly got a break in Vaudeville, billed as "Baby Carol." She was soon a big-time player, working alongside giants of the time. like Al Jolson, George M. Cohan, Harry Houdini, W.C. Fields, Eddie Cantor and other top acts. Her success gave her access to the best tutors. However, just as Carol, the pre-teen, was getting too old for her Baby Carol roles, so too was the audience outgrowing its interest in

Vaudeville. Carol and her industry hit the skids, and she joined thousands of other performers in the ranks of the unemployed.

Her mother, my Nana, was someone I got to know much later in her life. The Nana I knew had grayish white hair, fine and smooth. Her pale skin was thin and papery such that it revealed the blue veins underneath. Those submerged ropes of blue wound up and down her heavy arms and legs, exposed by the drooping sleeves of her fading pastel housecoat and her threadbare nylon stockings. Nana's face was round and wrinkled, and she was fond of flashing her nicotine-stained teeth in a happy-go-lucky smile, her soft blue eyes twinkling. You could see the love in those eyes for my sister and me, and we loved her back.

When she spoke, her words were punctuated by a series of small coughs, likely as a result of advanced COPD (Chronic Obstructive Pulmonary Disease) from years of smoking. When Nana was in her mid-sixties, she easily looked twenty years older. It wasn't just the constant ingestion of nicotine that advanced that process but the perpetual marination of her body in alcohol, mainly beer, that helped. When I met her, she was living with her daughter, Grandmother Noonan and her husband, the volatile and mechanically-inclined Mr. Edward Noonan.

Nana carefully managed her vices, always keeping them close: a lit cigarette in one hand and a can of Pabst Blue Ribbon in the other. The pocket of her housecoat was the repository of a variety of lurid publications, usually *True Detective* magazine or *Police Gazette*. The stories of crime and punishment drew her attention like a moth to a flame, and she devoured such publications with a passion. Had she lived until today, I'm sure she would have been an ardent consumer of reality television, like *Dateline* and *Cops*. Her small bedroom was stacked high with back issues and littered with doilies, framing the miscellaneous tchotchkes from her past.

Disowned by her mother in her youth, she had lost what could have been a sizable inheritance, but she never complained or made excuses for the choices she made in life. Early on, she had learned self-sufficiency, and it stood her in good stead when things got tough. Actually,

Nana had received some money, but it was more of a second-hand situation that benefited her. Her brother, William, had adopted Detroit as home and set up a hardware store business, Burns Hardware. Feeling far more compassionate than their mother, William invited his sister and niece to come to his new city and staked Nana to a small candy and ice cream shop. William's offer had come just in time for the desperate single mother who could no longer count on the money her child made in the entertainment business. Nana and my grandmother moved in above the shop. Carol literally grew up as a soda fountain girl.

***

Years earlier, Nana had made an arduous journey from Ireland at a very tender age, settling with her parents in Brooklyn, filled with hopes about her new country and the prosperity it promised. But despite the great hopes, life was terribly hard for immigrants, constantly under siege from bigotry. Breaking out of the pull of few jobs and low wages, sometimes seemed an impossible task.

Her father was a plasterer by trade, and he eventually got work and rose to the top of his craft. His work can still be seen in some of New York's finest buildings, including Carnegie Hall. The neighborhoods of Nana's childhood teamed with dirt poor but hopeful immigrants: European and Russian Jews, Irish, Germans and non-Jewish Russian. Typical of the time families were huge, it's not surprising that Nana had twelve brothers and sisters. Her father never missed a day of work with his sand and lime, pastes, adhesives, solvents and asbestos, nor apparently, an opportunity to procreate. Desperate to provide for his family, he worked so hard that one day he simply collapsed and died. He was not an old man by any measure.

Now a widow, Nana's mother deliberately set about raising her children with the business and organizational acumen of a CEO. She understood that she had a pretty sizable built-in staff of employees and decided to use them. She assigned Nana the job of selling apples, while she put the brothers, who were old enough, to work as Brooklyn news boys. The matriarch took in wash and did odd jobs while several of her other kids hawked kindling wood and coal found spilled along the railroad tracks.

Once back on their feet after the disaster of losing their primary breadwinner, Nana's mother happened upon a vacant store and formed a plan. She approached the owner with a deal: if he'd provide her two free months' rent to see if she could run a successful business, she'd pay him back if she could make it work, and he'd have a good rental customer. It might have been seen a sketchy offer with a lot of ifs and, had it been anyone else but Nana's mother, it might not have flown, but she was a resolved and determined woman, and she won over the landlord. He relented, and her little ice cream and candy venture made money almost from the start.

After a few years of success, the budding entrepreneur reasoned that expansion and diversification were the cornerstones of success, so she expanded the business to include hardware and other goods. Thus, against all adversity, the family became, by neighborhood standards, quite prosperous. In those days, each household of some means would designate a de facto "lady" of the family, a promising girl who was set aside like fine china and never dirtied her hands. "Promising" generally meant attractive looks and this chosen one would become an investment to be cultivated with the end goal of having this anointed one marry into another, hopefully even more successful family. This concept stemmed from old traditions that probably have infused just about every culture on earth, and old country Ireland wasn't immune from those institutions.

Nana, though the eldest girl, had already been tainted by the early survival years after her father's death and was seen as used merchandise, a worker bee, not a queen...or princess. One of her younger sister's became the chosen "lady" and got a free, or at least discounted ride. But, for Nana, the rest of her life she'd have to work for what she got.

And, yet, even after the sentence of grueling work, Nana sensed she'd eventually be denied.

Despite her long hours in the store, the reality was the store would someday be handed to her brothers to run when they became old enough. Early on, it was pretty clear for Nana that she was damned if she did and damned if she didn't.

Nana's big break came in the form of a poor but earnest man of Irish descent.

He courted her, they fell in love, they married, and then the United States entered World War I. He went off to war to do his duty, leaving his young bride behind to pine for him and keep the home fires burning, so to speak.

On July 18, 1918, in one of the first actions against the Germans by the American Expeditionary Forces (AEF) under General John J. "Black Jack" Pershing, U.S. forces engaged the enemy in the Second Battle of the Marne, a consequence of an offensive the Germans had launched a few days earlier. Nana's young man was part of that force. The allies decided on an early morning assault and caught the Germans somewhat by surprise. There were more than 7,000 casualties in the melee, with the Germans suffering more than 5,000. Sadly, Nana's husband was one of those who lost his budding life on that terrible day.

He never returned to his bride, buried, along with his comrades, at Château–Thierry, in northern France, outside Paris. The only good news was his wife, Nana, bore him a daughter. The bad news was it was some twelve months after he departed. While it had been a rather long pregnancy by any standard, the intervening full year since sexual contact between husband and wife strained even early twentieth century comprehension of human gestation periods, along with the damning evidence of my baby Grandmother Carol's coal-black eyes and black hair, which contrasted suspiciously with Nana's fair features and her dead husband's blonde hair and blue eyes. This had all the makings of quite a scandal during that time.

In disgust, Nana's mother disowned her.

Nana never admitted her indiscretion, merely offering, "God works in mysterious ways his wonders to perform." Hard to argue with that if you were a believer, but the more down-to-earth in their circle saw it simply for what it was, a young bride, lonely and starved of affection and human touch. Even if it was not the touching hands of her husband.

After being repudiated, it was pure chance that Nana ran off with a married Jewish doctor a few months later. This proved to be providential, maybe even a godsend for Nana, for the man truly loved her and took her all over Europe after the war. It was said that they traveled the Orient Express through France, Germany, Austria, Hungary, Romania and all the way to Istanbul.

This alien sojourn lit Nana's senses and gave her a tremendous lust and appreciation for life and the big, wide world that beckoned. It also apparently inspired a deep unslaked thirst—sadly, less so for adventure than fluids—and along with the cosseting ruling-class rail travel, helped her acquire her lifelong relationship with Sir John Barleycorn. Things must have spun out of control because the Jewish doctor left Nana and went back to his wife during the Roaring Twenties. Nana, now manless, like her mother before her, was left to raise her child by herself.

But not letting a little setback ruin her fun, Nana embraced the hard, partying Bohemian lifestyle that gripped much of Europe in the Art Deco Age and became a flapper, a fashionable young woman ready to flout convention and live life to the fullest. Nana was fascinated by the nightclub lifestyle, both for the excitement and also because that was where the booze could be found. It was then that she pushed her young daughter to take advantage of her dancing ability, and Nana became the twenties equivalent of what is now called in Hollywood a "momager." While my Grandmother Carol found success as "Baby Carol," all the dancing rage with the Hollywood elite, so too did her mother Nana find her true calling as a stage mother.

Nobody mourned the death of Vaudeville more the Nana.

***

Nana and her daughter Carol found their way to Detroit after the demise of their industry, and Nana, knowing the ice cream business, started her own little ice cream parlor in the Motor City, with her brother's help. Like her mother and her grandmother, my grandmother Carol learned the ice cream business inside out and was a young woman working in her mother's ice cream parlor when one day a strikingly handsome specimen walked in: a man with huge arms, barrel chest and those convex, penetrating brown eyes. Ed Noonan's dark, wavy hair and his smooth-as-grits-and-gravy Southern charm put him over the top with Carol. They fell in love and married.

Soon, Ed took his blushing bride back to Savannah with him where they planned to make their home. One of the outings they enjoyed was boating to Whitemarsh Island, in the Savannah River delta. They would make a date of it and put in at the island's only public landing and take walks around the island, which was a couple miles across. One day, while patrolling the shoreline, they saw a man nailing a big sign onto a tree on the property of a small house on the riverfront.

The sign said: *Bank Foreclosure. House and Property $12,000.00.*

Granddaddy beached his boat and excitedly ran up to the man.

"Take that sign down!" he exclaimed, "I'm buying the property!"

"Can't do that mister," the man said, shaking his head. "You gotta call the bank. I'll take it down when they tell me it's sold."

That did not fit the Granddaddy Noonan Spur-of-the-Moment Investment Plan, so he reached up, grabbed the sign off the tree with both hands and snapped it into two. He offered the man the pieces along with the ominous Ed Noonan stare. The man wisely beat a hasty retreat to his car.

Within a month or two, one Mr. Edward Noonan owned the house by the river. It turned out the property had a good story, the kind Granddaddy Noonan appreciated. The bank had foreclosed because the owners had embezzled a hundred grand cash and went to prison. The FBI had frantically searched the property, drilling holes through the house and yard, in a vain search for the dough. Though the place looked like it had been infested by a horde of groundhogs and pterodactyl-sized woodpeckers, Granddaddy wasn't gonna let that slow him down, and he and my grandmother moved into the house.

Granddaddy always suspected the money might still be hidden somewhere in his yard, an idea reinforced by the appearance of the embezzlers one day, fresh from jail and obviously looking for something. Riverfront property owners frequently added soil to their yards because the landscape changes frequently due to varying tides and storm-induced floods. The embezzlers began sneaking onto the property at night but were unable to find money. Granddaddy was not to be trifled with, and when he got wind of their missions, he chased them away with his twelve gauge more than a few times.

He figured they must have been serious to brave an angry man with a shotgun, but, try as he might, he never found any money on that property.

***

The times we ran away from Ralph and headed to Granddaddy Noonan's were like going to summer camp. I loved it. For a kid, I was in hog heaven. We were right on the river, and I loved playing with Granddaddy Noonan's mutts, Big Dog and Darn Dog, as well as the affable and barefoot backwoods kids, with names like Teanie, Desie and Boonie. It was all like a dream, given the hard life back home at the Calvert Street menagerie. What I did not know was that we were still in the presence of darkness. It's just that it was hidden from the eyes of a child.

Grandaddy Noonan was not only a serial philanderer but also as serious a drunk as Ralph or Jake ever were, and he regularly beat his wife, Carol, and his four children, too, when they were young. When I was there, he seemed to be a normal, loving man, and I had no clue about his psychotic behavior until I was well into adulthood.

He would wake me up at 4 a.m. sharp, good-naturedly bellowing, "Troy, c'mon and get up! I'm gonna fix you a Granddaddy Noonan breakfast!"

It was just the two of us in the kitchen while everyone else slept. He would drop several eggs into a big old cast iron skillet, filled with bacon squeezings, bubbling at around a million degrees, and they'd cook in what seemed like two seconds. They were ridiculously good.

Pat Conroy, future author of *The Prince of Tides* and probably a teenager then, lived across the river. My uncles always insisted that Pat Conroy would later use his father, Donald Conroy, to model the out-sized character Lt. Col. Bull Meecham in his novel, *The Great Santini*, but there was speculation from those who knew that Bull had bits of Granddaddy Noonan in his DNA.

Twice a month, Ed would travel by motor boat down to Daufuskie Island, which was just south of the famous Hilton Head Island, where his old, colored friend, "Two Times," had been running a well-concealed still for decades. Looking for a nice haul of booze, the trip turned out to be a great disappointment for Ed. Two Times was tall, stooped and white-haired. He shook his head sadly when Ed came up the crooked path.

"Say, Mistah Ed, got some bad news."

The old bootlegger pointed to the shed that housed the still and liquor inventory.

The hanging, busted door and broken padlock on the ground told the sad tale.

"State revenoo-ers done cleaned me out."

Ed gritted his teeth, sized up the situation and within ten seconds had an answer for Two Times.

"I'll rebuild ya the damn thing but ya gotta hide it better this time."

The men shook hands.

Ed then set to work on the apparatus in his spare time. Sometimes, he enlisted his son John to help. Ed took on the task in typical Ed Noonan fashion, which is to say he set about mastering the chore at hand: building a still. And given he'd never distilled anything, it was new ground. But Ed began to teach himself, through books and questioning those who did it, on everything you needed to know about distilling alcohol. It was important to him to get this right, not just because he was a prodigious customer but because he couldn't stand to not be the best at whatever he tackled, be it his factory, his Volkswagen Beetles or bus or now the transformation of water and grains into something that would fill his glass in the evening.

After doing his research, he procured a state-of-the-art vaporizer and condenser. Next, he manufactured a huge copper vessel which had to be ferried across the river. Then, Ed found four men, including John, to help him carry the new still deep into the heavy brush on the other side of the island. He spent a few days installing it and making sure it was working properly. Once it met his approval and he had it up and running, Ed and his friends could again be guaranteed a continuous supply of cheap hooch by their master distiller, Two Times.

Granddaddy was always larger than life to everyone, but especially to a young boy who looked up to him and revered him. He was a force of nature to me. But he was nowhere near as immortal as I had imagined him to be. Granddaddy Noonan was smart, very smart, but he eventually outsmarted himself and paid the ultimate price.

One evening after work, he brought home an impressive set of mechanical drawings and rolled them out in front of my grandmother Carol and her mother, Nana.

"The Southern Paper Board company is buildin' a plant in Ecuador, and I'm goin' there for three months to help set up the machinery!"

They were dazzled not only by the complexity of the drawings but by the fact Granddaddy was the guy chosen to make it all work. He packed his bags and took off the next week. There was only one big hitch to the grand scheme, and Grandmother Noonan and Nana were unaware of it.

It seems Granddaddy had fallen for this hot little blond waitress in town and devised a crackpot plan to be with her. Not only did he not go to Ecuador, rather he rented a cottage on Tybee Island (yes, where we accidentally dropped the H-bomb on ourselves) to spend time with the waitress between her shifts.

His nutty plan worked. For a while. Unfortunately, his machinations unraveled when by mere chance, a week later, he and his sweetheart stopped at a traffic light on Johnny Mercer Boulevard. The two lovebirds were unaware of their surroundings, and part of those surroundings happened to include Grandmother Noonan.

Apparently, this was not Granddaddy's first offense with his wife. They had argued this point before: Grandmother Noonan was understandably not so tolerant of other women in their marriage. But this was the last straw, given the wacky lengths he'd gone to buy time to get his trim on the side. The Ecuador Gambit was the last straw, and Grandmother Noonan put down her foot: Granddaddy wouldn't have to pretend anymore, because she was throwing him out of the house, and he could shack up with whomever he pleased without any pretenses.

Despite his guilt, Granddaddy would not be spoken to like that— aside from the fact he felt it was *his* house—and decided Grandma Noonan and, while he was at it, her pesky mother, Nana, would pay for his sins. In a fit of rage, he went to his truck to get his famous shotgun to end the lives of his accuser and her mother and continue living the dream with his blond cookie. Grandmother and Nana watched in terror as he went for the gun, knowing Ed Noonan was not a bluffing kind of guy.

Unfortunately for him and fortunately for Grandmother and Nana, in his blind fury, as he reached into the truck to get his weapon, he accidentally slammed the door on the firearm and, as loaded guns are wont to do when they are jarred, it went off. Sadly, for Granddaddy Noonan, his head was in the way and the blast ended the mad, brilliant, chaotic life of Edward Noonan.

Nana would later observe of her would-be killer, "That he looked so peaceful laying on the ground, like he was asleep."

Hard to imagine this calming image given the likely real estate missing from his noggin but, forget it Jake, it's Savannah. Nana also noted, and it was likely true if you're a believer and in the Deep South where it's hard to find anyone who isn't, "God saved our lives."

Ed Noonan died as he lived, in a flurry of rage ultimately tempered with an almost cartoonish irony.

CHAPTER SEVEN

Game Review

"Those who don't know history are doomed to repeat it."
—Edmund Burke

Grandmother Noonan lived another twenty five years after the violent demise of her husband. She left this world on an operating table in a Savannah hospital where she went to have a cyst removed from the back of her neck. Apparently, during the procedure, there was an accidental incision that caused her to lose a lot of blood, and she went into a seizure. I'm not sure how that can happen right there in an operating room but, perhaps even more vexing, was why my mother the fighter—and experienced nurse by then—did not take on the hospital with a huge lawsuit.

***

One thing you do from the get-go as an aspiring chess student is study the games of the greats. You study the great openings and the great gambits, but you mainly immerse yourself in the great games. You memorize the play of the giants, the Kasparovs, the Spasskys, the Fischers, the Alekhines, the Karpovs, the Laskers. You steep yourself in the history of the game for if you don't know where it's been you don't know where it's going—or rather you don't know where your own game is going. You stand on the shoulders of the giants to look over the fence into the ballpark to help solidify your game.

As a northerner, I've tried to understand the complexities of the Deep South, particularly Savannah, given its importance in my family history. Despite the amount of time I've spent there—even considering myself a sort of a cocktail Southerner because of the family—but, admittedly, its idiosyncrasies, from its culture to its customs and even zeitgeist, have often both charmed and baffled me.

In 1994, when I was contemplating writing this book, I was in Savannah for Christmas holiday and decided to spend some time alone on River Street along the Savannah River in downtown Savannah. I wanted to take some time, slow down in typical Savannah style and simply observe and attempt to define what it was about Savannah and the coastal South that made the oldest city in the great State of Georgia unique. I wanted to walk the path of my forebears, get into their heads, feel the humidity, inhale the smells, steep myself in what made Savannah Savannah and try to delve into what makes the people from there who they are. I know that Savannans prided themselves on their food, slightly slower pace and being just a bit more "Southern" than pretty much anyone else below the Mason Dixon line.

The sun had finally emerged from several days of cloudy, rainy skies, drying all the muddy pools. It was pleasant out, but I noted with amusement that many of my fellow strollers still held their coats or jackets in their hands, as if they didn't quite believe the weather had taken such a lovely turn. That perhaps told me something about Savannans' reticence to accept change...that maybe we'll just stick around and see if that's *really* gonna happen, 'cause, well, we got time.

I decided to pick up an espresso at Huey's and slowly stroll along Factor's Walk, where beautiful iron railings lined the building of the Savannah Cotton Exchange. A Boston architect designed the Cotton Exchange, a stately red stone and masonry edifice with greened copper trim, and it served as the nexus for the Southern cotton trade, with

Savannah the number two cotton port in the world, at least until the boll weevil nearly killed the cotton biz by the 1920s.

Cotton brokers, or "factors," as they were called, grew in the Antebellum South and, for more than a hundred years, oversaw the trading of some two million bales of cotton yearly. The area around the Cotton Exchange was called, "The Wall Street of the South," for a time, it was such an economic powerhouse. Many times, I had seen a prominent metal plaque on a post in a little garden park cordoned off by an iron fence in front of the exchange, but I had never taken the time to read it. Now I had the time, and I stopped and read it. The plaque explained the history of the Cotton Exchange building and how it was now housed the Chamber of Commerce.

Suddenly, a soft drawl interrupted my reverie of another era.

"Young man. Young man!" called someone behind me.

I turned to find a frail but dignified snow-haired man on one of the nearby benches. Next to him sat an even more fragile woman with silver hair and blue eyes. The two stared at me, expecting a response.

"Yes sir," I said, conjuring my best courtly Southern response. Had I been back in Baltimore, I might have just said, "What?"

"May I be of any assistance?" I continued with my courtliness.

I walked over to the old couple, and they slid apart, making room for me between them. The old woman patted the space, as the old man also gestured. "C'mon, son, sit on down heah."

I was well aware that Savannah had more than its fair share of eccentrics. Earlier in the year, I had read John Berendt's newly released bestseller, *Midnight in the Garden of Good and Evil*, and it was chock full of Savannan whimsy. New Yorker Berendt had been captivated by the many curious personalities in Savannah and wove them into his work, a mostly factual recounting of a murder among Savannah's monied. The book, of course, created a huge stir in Savannah's social circles. One reason was the writer had managed to so accurately capture the fraught, Gothic atmosphere of the place. The other reason, and this is a quote from one of the cocktail parties, was, "An outsider came down here and spilled the beans." Savannans clearly kept their family secrets close and didn't cotton to outsiders making them look less than put together and impossibly genteel.

I was usually very adept at avoiding entanglements with such people like panhandlers and the End-is-Nigh sign bearers, but that day I was feeling playful and exploratory and figured I'd play along with whatever the old couple's little charade happened to be.

I sat down between the oldsters.

"Ya'll a tourist, son?" asked the woman.

"Yes ma'am," I lied.

"Where're ya from?" asked the man.

"Baltimore, sir."

"Stuart C. Axlebond is my name," said the old man, extending his blue-veined hand. I gave it a gentle shake and introduced myself.

"And this, Mistah Troy Roberts, is my wife Grace," added the old man.

I gave a nod, noticing that, despite her obvious very advanced age, her eyes were beautiful and penetratingly clear.

There was a pause, and I stirred, as if to get up, but the old man grabbed my hand and stopped me, pointing his cane at Savannah's business district.

"You tourists wouldn't know about all this, but this city's been slowly dyin' for years," he told me, then adding vigorously, "Fo' years!" as if to punctuate the depth of loss. And while I may usually spell their speech with the letter "r," never once did I hear a hard "r."

"Yes, son, property values are dropping off," he admitted, and again, property was pronounced "propitty."

"There's vacancies all over. There's crime everywhere," the old man shook his head sadly for emphasis. "Yep, the city's all an illusion. Smoke and mirrors now. That's all. Just a few days ago, they murdered a friend of ours. He was the nicest man around. Could'nta found a nicer fella anywhere. He just loved to chat and help people.

And they just up and killed him. Barbarians I tell ya."

"Who are 'they' sir?" I asked, wanting to know who the barbarians were.

The old man ignored the question and looked at my empty espresso cup. "Why don't you come up and have some coffee? Grace and I'd love to have you."

Mr. Axlebond slowly got up from the bench.

Before I could say no, Grace had grabbed my arm and was leaning on me to get up. The old man led cautiously as I escorted Grace slowly along Factor's Walk. I was surprised when our journey ended almost as soon as it began, a stone's throw from the park bench.

As it turned out, thirty years earlier, Mr. and Mrs. Axlebond had renovated a spacious office on Factor's Walk. Above the office, in the loft, they had built an apartment.

We entered the office. A large conference table was in the center, accompanied by eight chairs. It was more modern and luxurious than I had expected it to be. The office looked rich. Above the table was an oil portrait of a much younger Stuart C. Axlebond.

"What business were you in, sir?" I asked, as I faced a huge window overlooking the Savannah River.

"*Were?*" asked the old man with the slightest mock irritation. "Ah'm still in business son," he added, as they both laughed. "I might be ninety-six years young, but I can still sell real-state." Again, it was not real *estate.*

"Although the business ain't what it used to be," he added with a tiny whisper of disdain. "Mattah o' fact, I've been losin' money fuh the last ten years," he added, almost as if bragging. "My eyesight is so bad, honestly I cain't tell what I'm buyin' or sellin'!"

They both laughed again. This time I joined them.

I was led to a stairway as the oldsters hopped on a little railed tram and began to ascend the wrought iron staircase. I followed as they slowly motored upward.

I kept thinking what I'd tell my wife Margaret. *Margaret won't believe me when I tell her about this couple.*

Mrs. Axlebond hopped off the tram and hobbled into the kitchen.

"How do you like your coffee?" she called over her shoulder.

I glanced at my watch. I'd already spent more time than I wanted with them.

"Listen," I tried to beg off, "I'm terribly sorry but I have to get going."

Mr. Axlebond pouted briefly then brightened. "Well you haven't seen a thing son! Folla me."

He led me to window which provided another sweeping panorama of the river. I could see for miles.

"Is that South Carolina?"

"Nahsuh, that's Hutchinson Island. Still Georgia. South Carolina's on the otha side of the island, beyond Little Back River."

By the way, Georgia was always pronounced "Jawhjuh."

"You know," I said, "I've always wondered why Savannah was built on only the south side of the river. Most big cities that have rivers are built on both sides, like Boston or Minneapolis."

"Well," said the old man, "There's a darn good reason. The otha side o' the river is low lands, not solid ground. Wouldn't take any development. Go right into the water, end of story."

It was a good answer. It was a true realtor's answer.

He led me away from the window and on a lightning tour of the bedrooms and bathrooms in the huge loft. Such as Mr. Axlebond could do anything resembling lightning.

"So," I had to ask. "How long you been in real estate?"

"Oh my, why as long as I've been married," laughed Mr. Axlebond. "And Grace and I just celebrated our seventy-second wedding anniversary. That, ah believe, is almost the diamond anniversary. 'Course, so's the sixtieth so that don't really mattah, does it? We got eight grandchildren and sixteen great-grand children."

He stopped to ponder the numbers and the history of it all.

"Les' see," he continued, clearly proud of the statistics. "I graduated from Georgetown in 1922. I was in school and missed France, thank goodness. The first job I had was with an appraisal office in Charleston. Then they sent me down to Hilton Head to negotiate with the colored families that owned land on the island. The first time they saw me I tell you they practically threw me off the island."

He snickered to himself, his memories still clear.

"But I was persistent. I kept going back. Had to. Grace was pregnant, and the office promised me a huge bonus if I could swing a deal. Couldn't miss out on that!"

He sat down in an old easy chair, its leather polished from decades of contact.

"After they'd run me off a few times, the black folk started takin' a likin' to me. I guess they just admired my gumption and stick-to-itiveness. I finally negotiated a deal, offering them a great price. Only thing is they had one stipulation: No paper!" he said, except his "r" was more an "ahh."

Mr. Axlebond paused for dramatic effect.

I interjected a guess, "They didn't take checks?"

He laughed. "Well, that's certainly what I thought. So, I organized a trip up there with boxes of cash. And I'll be darned if they didn't all just look at me kinda angry like. Believe you me, I was completely befuddled."

"They didn't want the money?" I asked, confused.

"Well, that was mah reaction, so I asked 'em *what's wrong?*"

"We told you we didn't want no paper!" they said.

That's when I got the gist of it and so me and my helpers hauled the boxes of cash away back to the bank and switched 'em out for pails of gold and silver coins. They seemed to be happy 'bout that. So, several weeks later, I dropped by to see how they were doing."

"We just fine Mr. Axlebond," they said "'cept we're getting awful tired standing guard over our treasure day and night."

"So, I took 'em all down to the bank and showed them how banks worked and set up all of their accounts. They put in their treasure and were happy as clams."

As much as I was bewitched by the story and the teller, I looked at my watch again, wanting to get on with my walk. "Wow, that must have been some experience," I said hollowly, then I started backing towards the stairs.

"Thanks again for the hospitality," I offered, "But I'm terribly late for my appointments."

"That's too bad, Mistah Roberts," said Mr, Axlebond, "'cause I got plenty more stories I can tell you."

Grace appeared from the kitchen with a tray containing a steaming pot and three cups. I shook my head apologetically, now slightly guilty.

"Some other time, perhaps," I said as I shook their hands and made my escape down the stairs.

"Don't forget to sign the guestbook!" Grace called after me.

I saw the book lying open on the conference table. I briefly flipped through the yellowed pages and noted names of people from all over the world. What a couple of characters they were. I took a pen and wrote *Troy Roberts, Baltimore, Maryland.*

In the space for comments, I wrote, "Enjoyed the chat," which I did.

Back outside, I made my way off The Walk and down some stone steps to River Street. I watched the waters of the Atlantic pushing back against the mighty Savannah as they flowed westward inland, mixing salt and fresh.

"Must be high tide," I mused, more to myself but a couple nearby heard, and the man nodded.

"High tide's near six foot. I hear in Alaska the tide's thirty foot on one side and a couple inches on the other."

I nodded. I didn't know that. That was the thing about Savannans: they were happy to casually trade trivia with strangers. It was a quality you rarely saw in a bustling Northern city. I thought of the Axlebonds and their unqualified hospitality. I was a stranger—they hadn't known me for five minutes when they were inviting me into their home for coffee and rambling stories about real estate transactions with people who found something as common as a bank account a revelation. More charm, but I wasn't sure what it meant.

Granddaddy Noonan was a product of this environment, and he was not what one would describe as a charming man. Sure, he was charming to my sister and me, but what about the hapless principal and the myriad of others he threatened and intimidated, including my mother, my grandmother and her mother? Charming, yes, at times, but a psychopath, too, and, while you can turn on the charm, you can't control psychopathy. I wondered about my own demons, my struggle with bipolar and how much of it stemmed from Granddaddy's genes. It was then that I knew I wasn't exploring Savannah to understand Savannah. I was actually looking for who *I* was, not who or what this city was. I wasn't here to study someone else's game—I was here to understand how my piece got where it was.

On River Street, I passed dozens of tourists with cameras, women with children in tow, merchants unloading goods on the piers. In the center of the river a huge container ship was making its way to sea. Also, on the water was a reproduction of a riverboat, probably off on an island tour. I mused that it was likely powered by a modern diesel, a fake sea-going Rolex with a Japanese quartz movement.

I breezed by shops selling T-shirts and souvenirs, such as kites and Confederate flags. I passed ice cream, confection and peanut shops. I thought of my family and their familiarity with ice cream shops, how they'd pulled themselves from poverty through ice cream and how my grandmother Carol had come to meet Ed Noonan in the family ice creamery. As I passed the shops, I wondered what dramas were taking place behind the scenes.

"They should put higher-class stores along this strip, it's so visible," I muttered to myself out loud then immediately chided myself for being such a snob and acknowledging that my irritation came not from the manner of the shops but probably from my own back story and my frustrated attempt to understand it.

I came upon the statue of Florence Martus, "The Waving Girl." It is a bronze of a young woman waving a large, billowing handkerchief (looked like a towel to me), her trusty collie at her side. The statue was erected in honor of Florence, who greeted every ship that entered the harbor at Savannah between 1887 and 1931. Her father had been a lighthouse keeper in Germany, and the family emigrated to the U.S., where her brother took up the family business and ran the lighthouse on Elba Island, between the main channel of the Savannah River and the South Channel.

I sat down by the statue's feet and looked up at Florence, faithfully waving to the ships, as they entered the channel. It was said that Florence nary missed welcoming an incoming ship and bade goodbye to the ones departing. Her extraordinary version of Southern hospitality filled me with awe. No one asked her to do this, yet, there she was, for forty-four years, greeting all the vessels as they came and went. What kind of dedication did that take? I mused on Florence's unselfishness and simple desire to just make someone feel welcome as they stood on the deck of their ship or on the bridge having made an Atlantic crossing or simply shuttled down the coast from Charleston. I thought about people like Florence and my mother and Grandmother Carol, on the one hand, and people like Uncle Jake and Ralph and Granddaddy Ed Noonan, on the other hand and had no answers. I wondered where I lay on the spectrum. I concluded that, by simply contemplating the question, left me a better person than the latter group.

I pondered the themes of *Midnight in The Garden of Good and Evil* and the dichotomy of Savannah. The genteel, almost loving hospitality and cordial pleasantry and then the dark heart of murder among the socialites and the unrestrained madness of an Ed Noonan. I decided Savannah was probably just like any other place.

I headed back toward Factor's Walk, thinking about my place on the chess board.

CHAPTER EIGHT

The Controlled Square

"The thing I miss most from home, is having a home."
—Anthony Liccione, Author

In chess, the controlled square is basically one over which you have dominion. I say *basically* since it is often a much more complex situation than simply a quid pro quo result, but for our purposes here I will stick to the basics of the concept. This notion of the safe or controlled square generally means you have a pawn or some other lower value piece occupying that square and, if someone actually threatens that square, you have another piece ready to defend it and kill that hostile piece, thus assuring you will cause your opponent more trouble than it is worth by exacting a higher price than they're probably be willing to pay to get it. With this predicament, you're giving your opponent a sort of a "buy high, sell low" paradigm. It would not be prudent for the other side to try and take that square since they'd lose their piece and come up with bupkis for their loss.

While North Calvert was a safe haven, to some extent—at least for two little kids and their mother— it was quite another thing. It often represented chaos and conflict on a scale that drove my mother to drastic measures. It was our frying pan and, with each episode we bolted, I'm sure my mother prayed we weren't jumping into the fire.

My mom and Ralph had a tempestuous, often explosive, on-again, off-again relationship. They were constantly breaking up, then reuniting, sort of like Europe in the first half of the twentieth century: warfare, peace, warfare, peace. Most of the time when war broke out, we'd flee to her folk's house in Savannah, but sometimes when staying with the Noonans wasn't an option, we'd head to Miami to get away from Ralph. My mother would find us a place to stay, and we'd try and settle in until the next round of return and departure came around.

During one such exodus, we found a quiet trailer park for solace, but Ralph tracked us down. He was so furious we had fled, he smashed his fists through the glass patio door after my mother refused to let him inside. He almost bled to death, he cut his hands so badly. I still remember the pools of blood on the patio, dark and thick, congealed almost like chocolate syrup and the ants that came by the tens of thousands to feast on it. It could have been just another disturbing image from some Italian neo-realist film from the fifties, but it was my life.

By the time we'd done it a few times, we had the escape protocol down pat. Mom would wait until the middle of the night when Ralph was sound asleep and would pack us up for the trip. We would carry our pillows and maybe a stuffed animal for comfort—fully dressed or in our jammies depending upon the urgency—and creep out to the waiting Caddy. For her, those moments between when she twisted that key, put it in drive and began to accelerate away were the most tense. Time ground to an agonizing molasses pace for her as she always feared he'd hear that big engine fire up and rush out and pull her out of the car. It wasn't until we'd cleared the first block down the street that she'd let out a deep, cleansing—and relieved—breath. Then she'd light up a menthol cigarette and put the pedal to the metal.

We would drive through the night to get to Savannah. She was manic, propelled by the ghostly image of Ralph pursuing us in the rearview mirror, spurring her to speed as she frantically put as many miles between us and him as quickly as possible. More than a few times, the police pulled her over for speeding, but she was practiced in using her beauty and feminine wiles to get off with just a warning and avoid alerting Ralph with a ticket on his car.

We were always safe at Granddaddy's as Ralph did not want to fuck with him. Ralph was a two-bit punk and a would-be hood and was comfortable pushing around the cretins he ran with and extorted for cash, but Granddaddy Noonan was a whole different animal to Ralph. In one of those instances when Ralph's instincts were accurate, he was correct in fearing a toe-to-toe with Ed Noonan and judging in his animal gut what a man like that was capable of doing. In Ralph's world, bluster and bullying got results, but he realized his father-in-law played by a different set of rules, ones that were so far outside Ralph's range of experience, he carefully—and wisely—avoided any interaction. He knew that Ed was volatile and deadly, having heard the rumors of Ed's impressive kill count during the war.

The chaos of moving around a lot put us in new circumstances, sometimes leading us into danger because we were unfamiliar with our surroundings. On one of our escapes, this time in Florida, a terrible thing happened to me when I was seven-years-old, and it would leave me scarred for many years. Perhaps even to this day.

My mother, needing money to pay the bills, placed Marie and me in a rooming house with a lady who fed us and gave us board, while my mother pulled double shifts at a restaurant. One day after school, I was playing football in the school yard with a few kids. I noticed, but didn't pay much attention to, an older boy of approximately seventeen or eighteen, watching us from out beyond the goal posts. The only impression I had of him was that he was overweight and tall. Though he lurked in the background, I was busy having fun and, while the big kid might have been a little creepy, he didn't seem out of the ordinary.

But, after our game, as everyone disbursed to their homes, he walked directly over to me. His face seemed impassive, and I wonder what he wanted since I didn't know him. He got right up to me, looked around, pulled out a knife, reached behind me and touched the point to the back of my shirt. I could feel the sharpness. It all happened so fast,

I didn't know what to do. My friends were now mostly out of earshot or vanished.

"Don't say a word or I'll kill you. Walk with me, and I won't kill you. You say one word, you're dead. You got it?"

I was so terrified I could barely nod my head. I dared not answer him lest he shove that knife into my back. We walked slowly to a house directly across from the schoolyard. Our footsteps had a weird synchronicity since he was a lot bigger, but I had to match his stride or anger him.

We entered the house, and he shut the door. Within seconds, he'd undone my pants and pulled them and my underwear down. I was scared beyond belief but also embarrassed. The knife still in his hand, he knelt in front of me, unzipped his own pants and exposed himself. Then, he put his mouth over my penis and masturbated. It didn't take long until he finished but it was an eternity to a seven-year-old. I could barely breathe. The experience itself was horrific, but I also had the growing terror he would end his monstrous act by stabbing me to death.

He pulled up his pants. "Where do you live?"

My mouth was bone dry. I normally could find my home pretty easily despite having just moved there but I was confused from my fright. I stammered. He put the knife to my throat.

"Take me there, you little shit. You understand?"

I nodded again, tears streaming, hoping this meant he wasn't going to slaughter me.

He walked me to the boarding house. I stood there, twenty feet from the door, twenty feet from escape from this demon.

"I know where you live now. Like I said, you say anything to *any-body* I'll know, and I'll kill you. Got it?"

When I didn't answer fast enough, he shook me. "Got it?"

I could barely whisper, "I got it."

The hours waiting for my mother to come home seemed almost as long and as emotionally charged as the lifetime I'd spent with the molester. I was gripped by stomach-churning terror as I obsessively looked out the window over and over, expecting that fiend to break in and murder me for thinking what I was daring to think.

My mother came home at approximately 1 a.m., and I ran and clutched her for comfort, frantically choking out my story in sobs and wet gasps. If he killed me, I wanted my mother to know who did it and why I died.

I will forever be grateful to my mother for the way she handled the situation. She'd had considerable experience as a victim and would be damned if someone would prey upon her little boy. She was loving and comforting but extremely determined, the latter quality she no doubt inherited from her father. As soon as she got me calmed down, she phoned the police.

At around two that morning, I led them to the infamous home across from the school. Several cops, hands on the butts of their service revolvers thunderously knocked on that door with the wrath of Thor, summoning all of the residents in a state of shock. Once they'd identified my dazed tormentor, he was cuffed and taken away, never to be seen again, at least in that neighborhood. He would go on to make a tearful, frightened confession and avoid a trial, but justice had been served and swiftly.

The incident was never brought up again by anyone. It was as if nothing ever happened, just the way I wanted it. It would be many years before I could purge the night terrors of those few minutes from my dreams, although once in a great while they play on the screen of my mind, but time has salved much of the distress I used to feel.

***

Whether it was the trauma of being molested or perhaps the strain of always being on the run, I'll never know, but what I do know is that, while hiding in Florida, I started acting out. One of my first antisocial acts was spray painting units in the trailer park where we lived. I was easily recognized, fingered and got in a lot of trouble but also got my mom in a lot of trouble for harboring such a miscreant child. I was very lucky not to have been arrested or sent into some sort of juvenile punishment hell.

But I didn't learn a lesson because next up on my crime spree was perhaps a weird homage to my family's history: shoplifting ice cream and candy from the supermarket. Then, I moved up to vandalizing gas station restrooms. I had decided I hated God and internalized this anger in my darkest thoughts and externalized it with the most expressive, misanthropic actions I could muster.

Perhaps existentialism was just too painful, and, with all of the shit raining down on me from every side, it was easier to just blame the man in charge, the Creator. I didn't have any real religious affiliation through my family, despite my Mom's mother being a hardcore Christian Scientist, but I understood the concept of a higher power and at that age figured it made about as much sense as anything else to explain who put us on this mortal coil to suffer like we did. So, as a child, I guess I pretty much summed it up as *thanks a lot, fuck you, and here's what I think.*

During my rampages, I would have something akin to an out-of-body experience, as if I were watching myself perform in a movie. I was a character in my own violent mind film, and I was merely following some malevolent but necessary and satisfying screenplay. Some kids pretended to be Batman or Superman, or these days, Spiderman, but I could become any renegade, felon or troublemaker I wanted to be, and I let my instincts write my parts. It was exhilarating and freeing to physically express the rage within me.

It was the beginning of the biochemistry of bipolar disorder expressing itself within me.

***

When the heat got too high at home, Mom would run away with us, and sometimes we would take up right under Ralph's nose. One time, Mom ran off with a hustler friend of Ralph's, and we holed up in rooms at the Mount Royal Hotel, literally across the street from Uncle Jake's place. It was weird fleeing across the street, given our flights were generally interstate, but the good thing at that hotel was that we always had room service. It beat the hell out of mobile homes.

We lived there until Mom finally caved for some reason and walked us across North Calvert Street back to Ralph. And so, the mad cycle of running and returning continued. Another time, Mom ran away and set us up in a fourth-story apartment above North Charles Street and East Preston Street, just four blocks from Uncle Jake's. Mom was working all day, and my sister Marie and I were left alone every day for an entire summer. The money from her job pretty much paid the rent and bought some basics but left absolutely no room for frills like a TV or air conditioning. It got suffocatingly hot in that place, but we were trapped since she'd forbidden us from leaving out of fear we would run into Ralph. The odds were high we would, given he spent a lot of time on the local streets hustling. There was nothing to do, and Marie and I would just sit for hours in the window sill watching the cars and people below. Sometimes we'd while away the hours by pitching cards into a hat. It was a sad way for kids to spend their formative summers, killing time, essentially prisoners in a fourth-floor walkup.

One day, near the end of summer, there was a loud pounding on the door.

"Open the goddamn door!"

It was Ralph.

He continued beating on the door. "Open the door, Troy! Open the goddamn door, or I'll bust it down! I have to do that, and I'll kill you! Open the goddamn door!"

Marie and I were petrified as he slammed the door so hard, I thought it would come off the hinges and then he'd kill me as promised.

"Open the door you little brat! Open it! Now!"

He pounded and pounded, and I could see the door was going to lose the battle. I took Marie's little hand as she whimpered in fear and guided her to the side window that led to the fire escape.

"Go!" I whispered loudly. She climbed out onto the fire escape, and I followed her. The problem for two young kids was that we needed an extension to be released to drop a ladder to the next level, allowing us to escape, and I didn't know how to activate it. We heard Ralph finally break in and cowered on the metal escape. He growled with rage and knocked stuff down and broke things searching for us. I looked at the drop to the street and actually considered whether we would survive it. I concluded we wouldn't. That's when he found us.

A hand shot through the window and grabbed my shirt. "C'mere, you little fucker!"

He dragged us both off the fire escape and proceeded to brutally smack the shit out of me. I know this is a saying, but in my case, it was actually true: I literally shit myself I was so frightened. It was even scarier than when I'd been molested, if that's even possible. Ralph savagely beat me—a little boy—in front of his even younger sister, until I passed out.

When I returned to consciousness, Ralph was busily frying slices of bread, coated in butter. He asked me if I wanted some as if nothing had happened. Neither Rod Serling nor David Lynch could have written a scene any more disconnected from reality.

***

Regardless of whether we hightailed it to Florida or Georgia or even across the street, the gravity of our circumstances always pulled us back to North Calvert Street. It was almost as if we'd throw our stuff in the car in the middle of the night and set all our hopes and dreams on reaching the moon, but we'd never quite achieve escape velocity and always fell back to earth or, in our case, the only earth we seemed to know, North Calvert. But there were some good times amidst the horrors and madness. One of the smells I carry in my head from the fifties and early sixties was the sweet, pungent aroma of Uncle Jake's El Productos as the cigar smoke would waft through the apartment and the hallways.

When I cleaned apartments with Uncle Jake, he would yell at me, "Two hands! Work with two hands!"

He practiced what he preached because he always had that cigar stub parked in the corner of his mouth to keep his hands free. It didn't take long until I made sure he always saw me with both hands in motion. And there was a big difference between Uncle Jake's yelling at me and Ralph's. There was some attachment to humanity with Jake's admonitions. He actually cared about me.

Sports at that time and place were huge. Religion was big, but sports? Well, you could pretend to be a Catholic or a Jew or whatever and just pay lip service to your beliefs during the week, but with sports it was serious. In Baltimore, it was a part of life that cut to the core of who you were and what you believed. I religiously played stickball in the alleys behind Uncle Jake's apartment building, and Uncle Jake and I would listen to Orioles home games on the radio and watch the away games on the tube.

Before I was even five years old, Uncle Jake taught me how to read the box scores of baseball games and make sense of the standings and batting averages in the newspaper. Uncle Jake had a gift for making even the simplest things, like eating crabs or strawberries or watermelon in his concrete backyard, something special, an event. We would take trips to Lexington Market to get ingredients for his legendary pasta dishes and, after repeatedly tipping the wine he brought along, he'd always be drunk by the time we got home.

He took me to my first baseball game. I'll never forget that magical feeling of walking out of the tunnel ramp at Memorial Stadium and my awe at encountering the magnificent, humbling scale of a real major league ball park for the first time. Even though our seats were situated behind a large pillar, so we had to crane our necks to see the action, it took nothing away for me, I was so excited. It was the Orioles versus those damn Yankees, and though we lost ten-zip, I didn't care. Years before I'd ever heard the expression, I was beginning to understand it was the journey and less the destination that was important. Uncle Jake taught me pride in our city, to love everything Baltimore. Uncle Jake and I were also crazy for the Colts and their living legend, quarterback Johnny Unitas.

I had so many memories of experiences with Uncle Jake—the kind a father and son have—because my stepfather, Ralph, was drunk and just checked out most of the time. Not to mention Ralph rarely missed an opportunity to beat me, using any flimsy excuse he could. I could see he enjoyed it, despite his saying otherwise and wondered why he always phonied up some hollow pretense for the beatings. If I'd been able to verbalize my feelings, I probably would have just said, *"Go ahead and just beat me up, you son-of-a-bitch. You know you enjoy it."* Ralph Juliano was a sadistic bastard.

I was eight when an older kid who was at least twelve pounded me after school, and I came home crying. When I told Ralph what had happened he beat me again, as if the bully hadn't done enough. Then he grabbed my ear and dragged me around the corner where the other children were.

"Where's the kid?" he angrily demanded.

I pointed, not sure who scared me more, Ralph or the bully. Turned out, it was Ralph because Ralph engaged in what the military called psyops—mentally breaking down a person by psychologically attacking them. Oh, and of course, the threat of actually attacking them.

He pointed at the kid. "If you don't go over to that little asshole and punch him in the face, *right now*, it's gonna be a whole lot worse for you when we get home. You got it?"

It was a perfect Hobson's Choice. Stay in the burning building and be immolated or jump ten stories and die on impact. I did exactly as instructed and walked over to the surprised kid and without any prelude or words just hauled off and punched him in the nose. To my astonishment, the kid burst into tears and ran home screaming bloody murder, his nose gushing red like a fire hose.

I guess in this instance Ralph did use tough love—minus the love—to teach me to toughen up and always get in the first punch no matter how big your opponent. This preemptive, feral, first-strike philosophy would help my chess game years later. Pre-emptive moves in chess accomplish several positives for the perpetrator. First, it establishes your dominance. It has tactical value. It can also encompass part of a larger strategy wherein you leverage your new reputation for dominance as well as your predilection for seemingly out-of-thin-air moves, which, of course, they are *anything* but.

***

As a kid in a world of chronic madness, many of the adults around us left my sister and me on the knife's edge, in a constant state of tension over what shoe might fall next. One day, after moving back from Savannah, I went to Rossi's place to play. Rossi was a Jewish kid whose father owned a candy store, and they lived in an apartment above his store. When I walked into the apartment, I saw many of our belongings, to my amazement. I had been told they'd been stolen and felt sad and wondered why anyone would take the black poodle lamps I thought were so unusual, having never seen anything like them. I'd also wondered what evildoer would pilfer our set of Encyclopedia Britannicas I used to enjoy browsing. And there, as the centerpieces of my betrayal, were our late sofa and end tables. Turns out, to get some ready cash for his booze, Ralph had sold all of our possessions to Rossi's parents when Mom, Marie and I had last fled to Savannah.

One of the things that deeply embarrassed me as a child was wetting the bed. I know now that bedwetting can be a sign of deeper psychological issues, especially a disturbance or trauma in the home. With me, you had a veritable deck of cards of bad choices and influences that could have caused a little boy to lose control of his bladder while he slept.

Ralph, of course, was cruelly disinterested in the whys and had even less interest in comforting a child over something that so clearly caused me stress. The fact was that Ralph was probably one of the main reasons I had the issue. No one wets the bed on purpose, believe me.

Ralph once took Marie and me to the Baltimore Zoo. Ralph couldn't just do something nice with the kids and leave it at that but, rather, had to ransack his good deed. At the baboon cages, Ralph sensitively pointed out their pink butts.

"Troy's ass," he shrieked in hysterics for anyone within fifty feet to hear, "is going to look like the baboon's asses soon if he doesn't stop pissing the bed!"

He thought it was hilarious, but it was also a very real threat barely concealed in his notion of a joking comment. I was mortified and wanted to join the baboon family.

One time after we made our regular return from Savannah, Ralph got fed up with the wet mattresses, so he threw away my mattress and had me sleep in the bathtub or on the linoleum in the kitchen. Like I said, one of the triggers of bedwetting can be stress.

I never once wet the bed at Granddaddy Noonan's.

The chaos and tragedy continued at North Calvert. Cora Lee and Peggy used to sit around the apartment in their robes, taking pills and reading literary excrement like *The National Enquirer*. One day, Cora Lee may have lost count of her pill intake and the barbiturates did their work and flatlined her heart and respiration. Her chalk-white body was carried out in front of me and a curious group of neighbors and kids. Of course, she was wearing a robe with nothing on underneath.

Not long after that, a showgirl named Pat was jilted by her lover, and to show him (what for, I don't know) she threw herself off the third-floor balcony. Surprisingly, she was more resilient than she realized and didn't die but rather ended up paralyzed from the waist down. Left in this debilitated state with limited use of her limbs, she felt she still had something to contribute and decided to dedicate her new-found respect for life to giving Uncle Jake blow jobs to keep the rent credit flowing.

Uncle Jake, as tight as he was with a buck, happily accepted her form of currency in the trade-out arrangement. However, after finding her new life's mission less rewarding than she'd expected, she finally successfully ended her existence by leaving the gas on in her apartment, Sylvia Plath-style.

Years before Lynyrd Skynyrd sang about the smell of death surrounding you, one jockey killed his girlfriend and cleverly stashed her corpse in his apartment closet. This was clearly not well planned, as she soon began to send off a lovely perfume that finally brought the cops asking embarrassing questions. The odor of a decomposing body is something you never, ever forget. It was absolutely the worst smell you could imagine and filled the building with an atmosphere of doom.

***

It was a hot July summer day in 1966 when Uncle Jake and Ralph had a terrible argument. They seldom argued but this one got ugly, even vicious. Ralph had heard of a potential sucker for the "Mr. Penn" score up in New York City. Ralph wanted to do the score alone. He was supposedly owed money from touting in New York and wanted to both collect and pull the Penn score on a sucker. He claimed the sucker as his own and was insistent he didn't need Uncle Jake's help to pull it off. One of the sticking points was he didn't want to give Uncle Jake a cut of the very scam Uncle Jake had taught him.

Uncle Jake couldn't get past the irony and outrage of Ralph's cutting him out of the grift. Uncle Jake also was adamant that the Penn scam took more than one guy. It also stuck in his craw that Ralph was chiseling him out of some extra dough, which Ralph certainly was. This last issue sent Uncle Jake through the roof. He felt that he was not only losing money with Ralph going rogue on him, but he was losing money on his own scam. It was a rage loop that Uncle Jake couldn't abide...or escape.

Uncle Jake's white-hot argument with Ralph went on for hours (fucking Italians!) with Ralph finally summing it all up with some uncharacteristic and remarkable insights into his actual motivation for the move.

"Look," Ralph said in a rare moment of calm, "you've got your apartment building. I want this score because I'll invest the take in an apartment building just like you've got, and then I'll be somebody and have something that no one can ever take away from me. I'll be just like you!"

This property ownership/personal responsibility argument took the wind out of Uncle Jake's sails so, against his better judgment, he grudgingly gave his blessing for Ralph to go up to New York City to try to score big alone. Ralph caught a train north with dreams of the big score and property ownership, just like Uncle Jake. For a jamoke, like Ralph, it was finally his shot at the big time, and he'd come back the conquering hero.

Uncle Jake well understood that aspect of Ralph's motivation but also knew Ralph could fuck up a wet dream, so he saw Ralph off with some trepidation.

Soon after Ralph arrived in New York, he phoned Uncle Jake to tell him he'd succeeded in fleecing the mark and had made a good score $25,000. Now his dreams of "being somebody" were coming to fruition. Uncle Jake, despite the misgivings and venom spewed in the dispute, had to acknowledge he was proud of his student. Ralph told Uncle Jake he wanted to stay in town and enjoy his big score but he'd back in the next day or two. Then, he promised Uncle Jake, he'd look into getting that property, *"just like you."* Uncle Jake got off the call with no small feelings of pride. He admitted to himself he had been wrong, although losing a piece of the score did chap his ass a bit.

Four days later, two New York police detectives came knocking on Uncle Jake's front door with a shocking story. Ralph, just as he promised, had gone out to celebrate his score "Ralph-style," which unfortunately meant getting his hands on some heroin. He just had the misfortune to do it in Sherman Square, a small public space also famously known as Needle Park. Not ensconced among the savoriest crowd, Ralph was found the next morning, laying on the curb of a Chinese restaurant across the street from the park, stone dead, his head caved in, his money gone. The police weren't sure what was used to kill him, but my mother was told it might have been a hatchet.

Ralph always had this premonition that he'd die at thirty-three and, like the outlaw he loved to portray, bragged to everyone that his lifestyle was going to cause it. He'd been exactly right. There had been some conjecture that, because the guy he'd cleaned out had Mafia ties, his death may have been a hit, made to look like he was rolled and killed, but in Ralph's case it was probably just a matter of making your own luck and Ralph's had almost always been bad.

My mother got in touch with the coroner and although it had been murder, in order to collect on his insurance policy, she pleaded with them to say Ralph's death had been some sort of hit-and-run accident. They finally did so but the ruse never worked out, as Mom never collected a dime from the insurance company—Ralph's mother got it all. Uncle Jake was sure that Ralph had also been in possession of at least $25,000 that undoubtedly went into the pockets of his killer or killers. Sadly, Ralph died as he lived, a big let down to those closest to him.

***

After Ralph died, it felt like the end of an era. Uncle Jake stopped hustling full-time and his crew eventually disbanded and went their separate ways. Jake's heart just wasn't in it any more. Losing Ralph, who was like his only son, albeit as troubled and disappointing as he was, presented a sadness that was almost too much for the case-hardened Jake Juliano to handle. But there was money to be made, suckers to pluck and Uncle Jake needed to keep some cash flow, so, as the mourning waned, the grifts marched onward.

Uncle Jake found a decent trade in occasionally buying and selling distressed (or hot) jewelry, finding the profits hard to resist. Aunt Peggy and he would also do insurance scams on grocery markets by pretending to slip and fall, get "injured" then sue. They always settled. Of course, this was before every store had cameras. Uncle Jake had a long list of crooked lawyers who were very good at squeezing the settlements, and they never saw the inside of a courtroom. With Ralph gone, my mother, now all of twenty-eight-years old, was a widow with two small kids and not a dime of that insurance money to help her through the tough times.

Despite desperately needing financial help, she rebuked Uncle Jake's offer to help and moved us out of Calvert to a place in Greek Town on Tolna Street. She was angry with Uncle Jake because she felt he was in many ways responsible for Ralph's death and now her loss of support. I think she was frustrated that the guy she really wanted to blame was dead, so she focused her anger on the only living player in the drama who was left.

Now, residing in a lower middle-class neighborhood across from the old City Hospital, Georgia sized up her options and knew she had few. With no education and pretty much only waitressing jobs on her resume, that was about all she could do to keep us afloat. Back then, rent was comparatively low but so were wages, particularly for a single mother who's only real demonstrated skill was fetching plates and drinks. My sister and I were left to our own devices as my mother worked double shifts at Bud Paolino's Restaurant on Lombard Street in Highlandtown.

Augustino "Buddy" Paolino was a decorated WWII vet who opened a small restaurant after the war that became the hot spot. Bud Paolino's Restaurant was the king of crustaceans in a city that ate a lot of crab. Sports superstars like Joe DiMaggio, Mickey Mantle and Hank Aaron liked to drop by when they were in Baltimore. Bud's specialty, heaping piles of steaming crab, guaranteed throngs of customers and kept Georgia busy waiting on them. With our mother gone all the time, my sister Marie and I became experienced latchkey kids. I enjoyed playing soccer and baseball with my Greek buddies. Despite their lower middle-class means, the Greeks tended to keep their heads down, work hard and not cause much trouble, so our neighborhood was safe, and we had fun. It was a quiet respite from the past whirlwind of conflict that always had seemed to envelope us.

Modern day parents will cringe at this, but we played in the underground sewers that wound their way to the old Baltimore City Hospital. The water was green and slimy, and we could only see with matches. We would occasionally come across something either unidentifiable or very stinky, but that was part of the adventure. When not exploring the sewers, we swam in the horrendously polluted Baltimore harbor, the outflow of the Patapsco River which surrounded the promontory that made up the south end of downtown Baltimore. When we swam, we made sure we wore our Chuck Taylor tennis shoes so as not to cut the bottoms of our feet on the debris field beneath us. As a riff on the old joke, it was slightly better than playing on the freeway. We were also troublemakers when we used the nearby Mount Carmel Cemetery as our personal playground, making games of toppling tombstones, defiling grave markers and mocking mourners.

My mother met an older Italian named Santos who swore to her he'd raise her kids if she married him. Having had such spectacular luck with men in the past, she decided a trial period was a prudent first move to see how we'd all get along. We moved into his house a few miles away in middle-class Rosedale. One afternoon, Marie and I were alone playing, and Santo's dog brutally attacked her, completely unprovoked and out of the blue. She was around eight. The dog was big and lit into my terrified little sister like a t-bone steak. I tried to beat the mad dog off with a broom, but he wouldn't quit. A neighbor heard the blood-curdling screams and rushed to the rescue, gun in hand. Coming upon the situation, he didn't hesitate and started shooting and fired his gun until the deranged predator dropped dead. Watching slack-jawed from a couple yards away, I felt it was a miracle none of the bullets hit Marie. That neighbor must have been a helluva shot. Or damned lucky.

When he returned and heard the harrowing story, Santos showed his true colors. With a lacerated and shell-shocked little girl hospitalized, his only concern was that the neighbor had shot his dog dead. He was pissed that the man had, according to Santos, just up and shot his poor dog for no good reason. Even at my age, I was incredulous that the man could say that, in light of the blood-splattered child as Exhibit A, his killer hound had been unjustly capped.

This was a rare time when my mother's judgment proved a good idea with her proposition of the trial period. Fortunately, Marie got patched up, and since we didn't have a whole lot of emotion invested in Santos or his home, plans to move were generated about five minutes after my mother got home from work. We moved out within a few days. My mother's breaking off with Santos had major implications though, mainly through losing her job at Bud's. Santos and Buddy Paolino were friends, and Santos badmouthed her.

But my mom was resilient and motivated and quickly took another job, this time foregoing slinging crabs to slinging drinks at a biker bar. There she met Sandy, a hulking badass in the Pagans motorcycle club. The Pagans had been formed in the late fifties in Prince George's County, just south of Baltimore and bordering Washington, D.C. Though a fairly new club, they were already expanding to territories outside the Baltimore area. One thing that was interesting about the Pagans was that they strictly rode Triumph motorcycles instead of the traditional Harleys of other gangs, like the Hell's Angels. Either way, they employed the same business model as most motorcycle gangs (just as they still do), which is a well-organized criminal enterprise posing as a club for motorcycle enthusiasts.

Sandy, the biker, was a trim little man who wore short-sleeved white shirts with pocket protectors, kept his hair crisp and short and carried a briefcase. Okay, seriously he was a frightening tower of corded flesh, around six-feet and two-fifty with piercing blue eyes and long blond hair. I'm not sure what it was about him that warned of trouble, the proliferation of fierce tattoos up his arms or the *"I'm gonna kill you"*

Clint Eastwood squint, but, if you didn't perceive the signs and decided to fight him, you would come away maimed, most likely with less of your physical person than when the fight began, whether it was an eye gouged out or an ear torn off.

Sandy was a very threatening person. In other terms, he was psychotic. Sandy also had an apparently Rasputin-ish resilience, having survived three separate shootings, not to mention being hurled off a third-floor balcony. Sandy had cultivated this personal mythology as being difficult, if not impossible, to kill, which gave him a mystique within his circle of outlaw anthropoids who revered such feats of survival.

After the biker bar would close, my mother and Sandy would often bring a dozen or two Pagans over to our little row house in Rosedale to continue the carousing. Our place went from a safe home to a living hell because of Sandy and the pandemonium around him. Sandy, to be charitable, was not a man cut out to be a father, let alone a member of even semi-polite society. Okay, not even *human* society. In keeping with his brand of anarchy, he brought his two pets into our house, a ten-foot boa constrictor and a skunk that would constantly raise its tail to shoot stink juice on you, despite having its scent glands removed. I hated his snake, his skunk and, more so, I really hated him. I made the mistake of talking back to him once and he grabbed me by the throat, picked me up with one hand, knocked the shade off a lamp and held the bulb to my eye.

"You ever backtalk me again, you little bastard, I'll burn your eyes out."

I was twelve. I believed him.

About this time, I actually found I had more to worry about than Sandy. Bowing to financial pressures Mom moved us back to one of Uncle Jake's buildings. My Jewish friend Rossi whose parents owned the corner candy store and, as I explained, half of our belongings, convinced me into going to a school near him in a black section of Baltimore named Pimlico, obviously near Pimlico Racetrack. The neighborhood had traditionally been all Jewish for many years until the great white flight of the late 60s and early 70s.

Rossi attended a private Jewish School across the street from Pimlico Junior High School. There was the Jewish Community Center next to Rossi's school. He talked me into attending Pimlico Junior High, so we could spend time at the JCC after school. What he failed to disclose, but I found out pretty quickly after enrolling, was that Pimlico Junior High was 95 percent black. I'm not prejudiced, but I knew that sentiment might not quite work in both directions, and I entered the school with some trepidation. My concerns were fully realized when, about an hour into that first day of school, I witnessed a big, muscular black teenager holding a much smaller, younger white boy upside down to shake change from his pockets. I had been abused and brutalized by a long string of pros, but I knew I was about to experience something brand new and probably pretty terrible.

I was right. I would get beat up at least once a week by a different group of black kids. When I was fighting one-on-one, I didn't do so badly, but those times were rare because it always seemed to end up being three or four (at least) that would start a fight with me, and I always ended up with the black eyes and busted lips.

I begged my mother to pull me out of Devil's Island Junior High School, but she refused. I tried to argue there was no way I was going to make it through the school year.

She held firm with that patented Granddaddy Noonan refusal to cave.

"You'd better toughen up Troy and stand up for yourself."

Sandy, being the socially responsible adult in the situation, suggested I take a metal pipe and knife to school with me. I refused because, even at twelve, I was smart enough to know such an action would be sure to get me killed or sent to prison, where I would be killed. As I sweated out my problem with no help from the parental figures in my life other than social Darwinist-informed vigilantism, a miracle happened.

A huge, extremely tough and completely formidable black kid, feared by all in the school, took me under his wing. His name could have been the Angel Gabriel, but it was actually Tyrone Jackson. An older teenager, Tyrone was built more like a lineman for the Colts. He was so feared that when a group of kids would start a fight with me all it took was the drop of a name. When the sharks started to circle all, I would have to say was, "My friend Tyrone Jackson will want to know about this," and their faces would instantly shift from angry to quizzical to fearful.

"Shit, man, you know Tyrone?" they would ask every time, as if I'd invoked some black Voldemort.

"Yes," I would nod confidently and that would be that. They'd dissipate like smoke in the wind. I made it through the school year with Tyrone's powerful wings shielding me from further danger. The next year I enrolled at Robert E. Lee Middle School in South Baltimore where the racial mix was 70 percent white, not too surprising, given it was named after one of the favorite sons of the Confederacy. It was like I had died and gone to heaven, and my constant state of alarm lifted from me. I still stayed friends with Tyrone but no longer needed his protective shadow over me.

***

My mother had an Italian friend named Mario, a former grifter and who had hustled with Ralph. But Mario had since experienced a moment of clarity and decided to leave the life of crime and swindling he'd followed for so long and pursue a new, straighter path. Mario's answer to turning his back on his old life was to become a Jehovah's Witness. Like most religions, Jehovah's Witnesses feel like they have a better way and their church and belief system addresses and cleaves to the original precepts of the first century Christian church. They believe that Jesus Christ is God's only direct creation and that everything else is created by Jesus, God's only son, in service of his father and using his father's power. They also believe Jesus delivered us from our sins through his crucifixion but nit-pick the cross on Golgotha part of the story and acknowledge he was crucified but it was just a post. This flies in the face of historical crucifixions that did use crosses, but it's their story and they're stickin' to it.

I had known Mario awhile and remembered first being aware of him when he'd tried to convert my mother by offering us Bible studies at home right after Ralph was bumped off. We weren't interested then, but now with a crisis on her hands—whether to keep her son...or the psycho biker—she called Mario and asked if I could live with him and "get him some religion." Mario was a big-hearted man, and all too happily agreed to take me in and get me out of that dangerous environment. More suited to doing good than mischief, Mario was a handsome man with black wavy hair who was fully, unequivocally into his religion. But unlike many flawed hearts who wrap themselves in theological dogma for show, Mario was truly a sincere, budding spiritual being. He loved Jehovah deeply and the way he lived his life was a deeply honest testimonial to that commitment.

Mario owned a sub sandwich shop in Mount Vernon near the Belvedere Hotel and put me to work there in between my meetings at the local Kingdom Hall of The Jehovah's Witnesses, or my time spent studying the Bible. In his mid-thirties, Mario had remarried, and his new wife was a twenty-four-year-old knockout named Angela. She was, without a doubt, one of the hottest women I'd ever seen and hands down far sexier than any stripper roosting at Uncle Jake's. Angela was a white girl with the bountiful ass of a black girl that might have induced a gay man to go straight. When she was in the bathroom showering, sometimes I would sneak up to the bathroom door to try and get a glimpse through the keyhole as she dried off. Angela was beyond an adolescent's fantasy—she was off the charts to me.

Angela popped out two kids in the next two years with Mario's assistance. They kept me busy, always helping with their kids or doing my duty at the sub shop. My school attendance began to suffer because

Jehovah's Witnesses believed the end of the world was coming in 1975 so what the hell was the point of wasting your time learning stuff when it would soon all be over? It was the best excuse a high school kid had ever heard to avoid school. I also had even more work when Mario started a business delivering washers, dryers and refrigerators for Montgomery Wards. I ended up working almost full-time on the delivery trucks and completely quit school at fourteen. In my spare time, I would go door-to-door, pitching the Jehovah's Witnesses two most important publications, *The Watchtower* and *Awake!* To this day, *The Watchtower* is the most widely distributed magazine on earth, with more than forty-five *million* copies per *month!*

I eventually taught Bible studies and then moved up to giving sermons in front of the congregations. Mario and I created a nice bit of a backstory for me that had me "leaving my family to serve Jehovah" and this proved an inspiring and uplifting piece of fiction for the brothers and sisters of the congregations. It gave me a certain cachet with the church's regulars for having been a true soldier for Jesus. What greater love could you have for our lord than to have left your mother and sister to serve Him? Religions *love* sacrifice.

By 1972, there were only three years left until the battle of Armageddon, when God's chosen people (i.e., the Jehovah's Witnesses) would inherit the earth. In the battle where the righteous, led by no less an elite military strategist than Jesus himself, would defeat the profane, and there would be one thousand years of peace. At the end of the period of peace, Satan would get one more shot at corrupting humanity then peace would reign—that is, if humanity rejected Satan's game plan. I was pulling harder for us and Jesus against Satan than I ever did for the Colts versus the Redskins. It was a powerful rivalry and meant all of our souls. I believed in it all, that is until something else came into my life to "save" me from the rapture.

CHAPTER NINE

Ten Moves Deep: My New Religion

All I want to do, ever, is play chess.
—Bobby Fischer

The year 1972 was a milestone for me because it was the year I began to stray from the church because I found another, far more compelling religion: chess. This was the year the brash, outspoken American Bobby Fischer played the Soviet chess champ, Boris Spassky. The 1972 World Chess Championship in Reykjavík, Iceland, had stakes far more elevated than just two guys meeting for a board game. The Soviet champion, Boris Spassky, was a powerhouse player and the defending world champ. His challenger was a young, brash American who didn't always treat the stuffy world of international chess with the gravitas that made many of the establishment comfortable.

The match also represented a huge point of honor for the Soviets who viewed their autocratic stranglehold on the upper ranks of world chess as a clear demonstration of the intellectual superiority of the Soviet educational system. The Soviet's cerebral jingosim had parallels with the 1936 Olympics when the Third Reich sought to reveal their Aryan magnificence to the world by crushing everyone in their path. A humble but speedy black man named Jesse Owens hadn't been reading their press clippings and wrecked that little pipe dream for Herr Hitler.

Bobby Fischer was no less an iconoclast if nowhere near as mannered a winner as Mr. Owens.

If there was ever a smack talker in chess, it was Fischer, and he gave the Russians fits with his denigration of both Soviet chess and their political system, which were so strongly connected as to be indistinguishable. My interest was not only riveted by the titanic conflict between the two men, but my embrace of the game itself was beginning to blossom. I knew the game and felt an affinity for it, but it was during that time I realized I just might be good at it. I followed the match between the young American Master and the seasoned Soviet Master like a hawk and became obsessed with chess in true bipolar fashion.

I was soon devouring every book on its history, the history of all the great Masters and their games and set about studying chess with same fervor I'd studied the Bible. Only the difference was with chess I saw a future because there was nothing out there that said chess would cease in 1975. Most chess Masters usually learn the game forward and backward no later than eight-years-old, but I now knew what I really wanted to do and that was to become a chess Master, and nothing was going to stop me. I was sixteen, an elderly man in chess terms.

Of course, chess was frivolous to Mario and Angela, because they didn't understand it. They saw it drawing me away from Jehovah and had a number of concerned talks with me about false gods and so on. I knew what I had and paid them no mind, deciding to better deal Jehovah for chess. I left Mario and Angela's place and moved in with Uncle Jake and Aunt Peggy back at 1315 North Calvert Street. Yes, it was retracing my history, but I was bordering on adulthood and now making my own decisions. I was also gambling that the world would stagger on past 1975, because I threw Jehovah out the window for the greatest game ever invented.

***

Uncle Jake rented me a small room with a kitchenette on the third floor of North Calvert. I shared a bathroom with three other renters. Uncle Jake charged me ten bucks a week rent, which even in 1972 was a good deal. Since Uncle Jake had stopped hustling, to support myself I had to find a real job, and I made the tough decision to become one of his reviled lunch bag men. I took a job working at a necktie factory in the garment district down on Eutaw Street for a buck seventy-five an hour, which I believe was fifteen cents over minimum wage. I toiled at a mind-numbing task where I would stomp a peddle on a machine that pressed a small clip onto the neckties, a manufacturing trick that saved some clod the fifteen seconds it took to tie a real tie. I hammered that press peddle minute after minute, hour after hour, day after day, until I felt I would lose my mind.

I was also pretty much the only male at the garment factory, and I was surrounded by row upon row of black women sewing and stitching the ties on extremely long tables. A few of the women took a liking to me and brought me soul food like hog maws and chitterlings for lunch, but I was too young to realize they were sweet on me.

At night, my time went to studying the games of Bobby Fischer and Victor Kortchnoi to get ready for my first chess tournament, the Baltimore Open in 1973. In that tournament, at the age of seventeen, I scored 2-1/2 points out of five rounds (one point for a win, a half point for a draw, zero points for a loss). I earned a United States Chess Federation rating of 1275 and became a class "D" player (the average rating for a United States Chess Federation member is approximately 1300). To become a chess Master, you need to earn 2200 rating points. The rating system is approximately like this list:

2500 points and above plus norms Grandmaster
2400-2499 points plus norms International Master
2200-2400 points: Master
2000-2199 points: Expert
1800-1999 points: Class "A"
1600-1799 points: Class "B"

1400-1599 points: Class "C"
1200-1399 points: Class "D"

1199 points and below: Class "E"

You gain rating points by winning a rated chess game and lose rating points by losing a rated game. Today, there are almost 60,000 active rated tournament chess players in the United States. The vast majority of players spend their entire lives playing tournament chess and never get as high as 1600 rating points or class B. By continually playing in local tournaments and studying the games of the greatest players, I managed to push my rating to over 2000 by the time I was twenty-two. I made Master at age twenty-four.

My highest rating achieved at age thirty-one was 2339 putting me above 99.4 percent of all rated tournament level chess players in the United States at the time. I am living proof that if you have intelligence and drive, you can accomplish practically anything you set your mind to, no matter how late you start in life and no matter how many bikers and abusive Mafia thugs and molesters they throw in your way.

***

By this point in my young adulthood, I had been experiencing the effects of bipolar disorder for quite a few years, but having never been diagnosed, and this being the seventies, while more open-minded than the fifties, there still wasn't much awareness of the disorder which could have meant concrete help. It was still generally referred to as "manic depression" and people were often encouraged to just "deal with it."

Even today, approaching our third decade into the twenty-first century, the National Institute of Mental Health (NIMH) estimates that less than forty percent of people with bipolar receive "minimally adequate treatment," because of stigma, lack of funding and, perhaps worst of all, the public's lack of understanding (read: education) about the disorder.

The deep depressions I'd been experiencing for so long often shattered my life, but now something new and insidious entered my world. For the first time, I reached a point where I felt so far down in the hole of despair that there was no way out but one: suicide. I'd never tried to kill myself but had certainly thought about it a lot. As I got older, my thoughts became more formed about how to do it, as the depression rolled over me like white hot magma.

One evening, it got to be too much, and I gave in to my thoughts and plans of how to kill myself and decided to actually do it. I'd thought about shooting myself but had no gun. I considered taking pills but had no pills. I was smart enough to know that humans need oxygen to live so depriving myself of oxygen would achieve the desired results. I turned to my gas oven in my third-floor studio apartment. I knew that it had worked like a charm for that poor woman who had lived in my building as a kid. I blew out the pilot light and cranked up the gas and went to bed, expecting to wake up deader than a doornail. I fell asleep tormented by my depression but with the tattered hope that my misery was at an end.

I woke up, and it was daylight. Clearly, I was alive. I had a headache but that was about it. I staggered to my feet, the depression somewhat abated, and opened my windows and shut off my oven. My suicide attempt had been a failure. Fortunately.

It was weird, but as the day progressed—and my headache faded—I had a new-found appreciation for not being dead and began to make solid plans for my future. Making an extreme choice like suicide—then failing—woke me up to the possibilities and what-ifs when I realized I had a second chance. This can be inspiring or depressing, depending upon your perspective. I was fortunate that my failed suicide attempt had triggered something in me that gave me the will to choose to be inspired. It set a new standard for decisive action in me since I had "cheated" death, more or less. I felt freer to do what I was probably supposed to do without fear of repercussions.

I made a calm decision to quit the tie factory before I went nuts on that press. I walked out of there feeling liberated but also wondering what would come next since I had no backup plan. But leaps of faith often leave you asking that question until the answer presents itself. With an open mind, I went out looking for a job and found something that would turn out to be an enormous influence in my life. In fact, it still informs my career now, more than forty years later.

Albert Gunther & Co., at the corner of Biddle Street and Maryland Avenue, was Baltimore's premier hardware store. Occupying an imposing three-story brick structure, it was what remained of four of eight row houses originally built there between 1868 and 1869. Gunther's sold decorative door accoutrements, commercial door hardware, tools and every bit and piece, nut and bolt and nail and screw known to man. If you were in search of some esoteric fitting or fastener or object, Gunther's was the place for you. While Lowe's began in North Carolina, the year after WWII ended, and The Home Depot didn't begin operations until 1978 in Atlanta, neither chain had begun its nationwide conquest of the hardware world back then. In the seventies, it was the neighborhood hardware store that would meet the needs of the small contractors, remodeling bathrooms and creating additions, and the weekend warriors who wanted to build decks or install sconces in their hallways. The independent hardware stores had been the heart of American building-and-home improvement for more than two centuries and Gunther's was Baltimore's go-to institution for your domestic needs.

By the time I walked in the front door looking for a job, Gunther's had been open for seventy years, weathering two world wars and the Depression. Founded in 1907 by Frank Gunther, it took up an entire block and was considered the premier outlet for everything from contractor-grade merchandise to high-end home hardware.

I asked the first clerk I saw if the store had any kind of openings for work. They paged "Little Harry," a tiny, serious man who arrived in enormous Russian boots. He furrowed his brow, looked me up and down and nodded curtly.

"You'll do."

I didn't even get a chance to say, *"I was suicidal the other day but have a new-found respect for life and want to start over. And I'll work hard."*

That was Little Harry's style of a job offer, and I happily took it. I started in the shipping department at $2.50 an hour. The place had about a billion moving parts, from screws to light sockets and circular saws, but I made up my mind to figure out where each thing was located so no customer could ever stump me. I eventually got there, but it took a *long* time.

One evening, on my way home from work, I passed a building across the street from Uncle Jake's called The Fellowship of Lights. It was a place for runaway kids aged twelve to eighteen. Perched on the steps was this strikingly pretty girl with jet black hair and marble white skin. Honestly, she looked like Snow White, only a sad, bored Goth-version of the fabled character.

"Hi," I said, to break the ice.

"Hi," she replied wistfully, but, nevertheless, subtly inviting. I could see she wanted to talk to someone.

"I'm Troy. What's your name?"

"Lucy."

"You okay?" I had to ask, since she seemed so down, and, if there was anything I knew, it was down.

"Not really."

"How old are you?" I knew she was young but couldn't even get a range by looking at her. She could have been a mature twelve for all I knew.

"Sixteen."

"So, what's up?" I sat on the steps next to her, given we were now having an official conversation.

She paused a long moment and gathered her thoughts. Whatever it was seemed painful.

"Okay...I had this boyfriend. We were pretty good together, and I brought him home, and things seemed fine for a while. Then, I find out he and my mom are fucking."

Her voice trailed off with a sigh. I didn't dare say a word at this point.

"Anyway, so now they tell me, my boyfriend and my mom, that now they're in love. Crazy huh? So now my dad finds out and goes ballistic and tells my mom to kick Sean loose, and she says no, and she and Sean book and..."

Tears began to well in her eyes. I could barely breath. I held my breath, not wanting to disturb a molecule of air given the weight of the moment and what might come next in her story. I knew it wouldn't end well but truly wasn't prepared for her grotesque punchline.

She wiped her eyes. "My dad killed himself. Hung himself in the closet in our foyer."

I continued to hold my breath. I'd been through some shit, but this was stunning even to me. With her mother having run off with her boyfriend and her father killing himself over it, no one could fault Lucy for running away to seek solace in the Fellowship of Lights. As I pondered her astounding tale of betrayal, I realized she hadn't so much run away, as her family had run away from her. I felt an immediate bond and closeness to her. I saw us as two war veterans, a pair of survivors from separate fronts of domestic terror.

I asked if she wanted to go see *The Exorcist*, playing at the Morris Mechanic Theatre downtown on Charles Street. Nothing like a little supernatural possession and soul-gripping horror to take one's mind off troubles. After the movie, we went up to my room and started fooling around on my bed. Suddenly, the bed collapsed, which scared the total bejeebers out of us, especially after having just come from *The Exorcist*. Once we realized what had actually happened and that we weren't targets of the forces of metaphysical evil, we laughed our asses off.

***

After a few weeks of dating and pretty much wall-to-wall teenage sex, I asked Lucy to move in with me. Uncle Jake gave us the basement apartment for twenty bucks a week. The basement apartment was a big step up from my little room on the third floor with its shared bathroom. This place had a full kitchen and its own bath. It felt like The Ritz. A few months into our adventure, Lucy told me she wanted to get married. She was sixteen, I was seventeen. Being semi-responsible adults and more or less of sound mind, Uncle Jake and Aunt Peggy expressed to the semi-adults, with no lack of certainty, that we were nuts and they were dead set against it. I came to my senses and saw their point. I made the call and told Lucy we were too young.

Lucy's counterargument came a few days later when I arrived home to find her on the bathroom floor, barely conscious, her wrists slit and blood everywhere. She survived and, after three weeks in the psychiatric hospital, she was released. My next move was a colossal blunder you'd never *ever* do in chess but certainly one you'd do at seventeen: I married her.

Lucy got a job as a waitress at a restaurant across from Gunther's Hardware. We were relatively happy. To keep her thoughts from the dark side, we enrolled Lucy in ballet classes. Turns out she loved ballet. As a child, she had dreamed of being a ballet dancer, so this seemed like a good fit. I continued to study chess, played in tournaments and grew stronger as a player. I was thrilled when I won the prestigious Towson Chess Club Championship. As my need for stronger competition grew, I started playing at the Catonsville Chess Club, a notch or two above Towson in skill and experience. Then, I went on to win the Catonsville Chess Club Championship two years in a row. I won many local tournaments, I was on my way as a chess player. Lucy and I were actually happy despite living paycheck to paycheck. We didn't even have a checking account, but it didn't matter.

Then, disaster struck. Again.

One afternoon, while I was at work, Lucy came home from ballet class early and, instead of entering our apartment from the front entrance on Calvert, she came in from the back alley, directly to our basement door. A very tall, black man came up from behind, dragged her into the apartment and proceeded to rape her for hours before finally letting her go before I got home. The incident left her completely rattled and on edge. She was never the same after the attack and who could blame her?

A few months later, Lucy spotted the rapist on Eager Street near our apartment and called me at work, barely able to speak, she was hyper-ventilating so badly. I raced home, grabbed her, and we ran to the street and flagged down a cop. By then, the guy was gone, but we knew he was close by and did not know his victim had recognized him. Lucy gave the cop a breathless description, and the cop quickly wrote down everything she said in his notepad. Then, he had to make a quick decision whether to drive east or west in pursuit, since Lucy was so jarred, she could not recall which way he went. A mixture of rage and racism bubbled to the surface when the cop observed, "Niggers always run to the eastside," and took off that way.

Racist or not, his instincts—or luck—paid off, and, a few blocks later, the cop apprehended the rapist. We later found out he had been on work release from the penitentiary and was walking back to the prison. The cop arrested him one block from the pen. We went to trial, which was an ordeal for Lucy, but we got a conviction, and the rapist was sentenced to thirty years. However, our marriage was never the same. Lucy and I grew distant, as our sex life was not the same, and I grew bored because of my bipolar condition. As much as I missed sex, and it was a large part of our relationship, especially at that age, in my heart I knew I couldn't push her to do something that now reminded her of the unthinkable. Some injuries cause a body part to break or go missing and some injuries cause a part of your soul to die. The latter happened to poor, sweet Lucy.

***

The brutal, hours-long sexual ordeal left Lucy frightened of our basement apartment. She developed a fear of black men and insisted we move away from our integrated downtown Baltimore neighborhood of Mount Vernon. Lucy's mother and ex-boyfriend were in the process of losing their small row house in South Baltimore, a white working-class neighborhood south of the Inner Harbor. This was long before Yuppies discovered "SoBo," as it was later called, but, at that time, it was a tough, poor part of town. It was also lily white, and that was all that mattered to Lucy.

To buy Lucy's mother's house on Barney Street out of hock from the bank was going to cost eighteen grand, and I needed five hundred dollars down. I was making a little less than five bucks an hour, so I clearly didn't have the cash. I asked Uncle Jake. True to his habit of never loaning anyone money, he stalled me for several weeks while the bank's interest rate was rising. Frustrated by Uncle Jake's dancing around the issue and, with pressure to close the deal and rescue my tortured wife, I finally screwed up my courage and asked my boss, Frank Gunther Jr., for an advance on the down payment cash. He gave it to me in an instant. I almost cried at his generosity and big heartedness and couldn't help but compare his no-strings largess to the cynicism and tightfistedness of my family. But Mr. Gunther treated his employees like family and was both truly kind and a gentleman. These were probably two of the million-and-a-half differences between Uncle Jake and him.

***

Apparently, despite the mythology that he was somehow immortal and impervious to harm, despite his numerous gunshot wounds and being hurtled down three stories, Sandy the biker finally succumbed from complications of a fourth and final gunshot wound. Perhaps such a life-altering event gives one pause to reflect, and my mother gave up alcohol and went back to school. At 34, Mom decided she was too old to be a waitress or barmaid any more, but, truthfully, she was tired of it and wanted something more. Mom was a late bloomer, like Grandmother Noonan, who had gone back to college to get her master's degree in mathematics at the age of 44. Back in the fifties, advanced degrees were not that typical for women. The old stereotype back then was that women went to college to get their MRS degree. Not so for Grandmother Noonan who was valedictorian and made the Savannah newspaper for doing so. All that with Ed Noonan as her husband. She should have been given an extra degree just for that.

As Mom sought options for relief from waitressing, a social worker told her that nurses were in high demand. She decided that was a career with weight and integrity and one she would pursue. She told Marie and me that she was going to be a nurse because she wanted her kids to be proud of her. Her first step on her journey toward realizing her new dream was to earn her GED. Once she had her high school ticket, she enrolled in a two-year course at Anne Arundel Medical Center and became an LPN.

Ten years later, she went back to school and became an RN. After twenty-five years as a registered nurse, she finally retired in 2009 at age 72. Over the years, she worked at many hospitals, in Maryland and places like Connecticut, and did her time in cardiac and burn units. By the time she hung up her stethoscope, she had helped countless people over many years of selfless, difficult work, receiving far less appreciation than nurses so rightly deserve. She was a big help for this book, piecing together many details, and I also asked her to share some humorous stories from nursing.

She quickly shook her head. "No, Troy, there were no funny stories, just death and gloom." So, no funny hospital stories.

My sister Marie followed our mom's footsteps and also became a nurse.

***

There I was, twenty-three-years old, owner of a small two-story house in one of those parts of Baltimore with redneck, white-on-rice non-diversity and married to a young, frightened woman who had become like a roommate with no benefits. South Baltimore was a tough place full of rough-and-tumble people. Men beat the crap out of their wives, and, when the cops came, they beat the crap out of the cops. It was an urban Thunderdome with pleasant street names like Clement and West and Light.

Mostly for show, and to reassure my jumpy wife, we got a medium-sized mutt and kept him in the tiny back yard. I named him "Spinks" after Leon Spinks, the boxer who pummeled an aging Muhammad Ali. Unlike Mr. Spinks, the human boxer, Mr. Spinks the dog was not only not a boxer but was all bark and no bite, harmlessly yip-yapping at anyone passing in the alley. He was our poor man's motion sensor. One day, I heard Spinks whimpering, and a young man around my age yelling at him. I went out back and was stunned to find the guy beating Spinks with a large stick. Furious, I jumped the fence and punched him in the face, knocking him out colder than a mackerel. He lay there for a few moments, then finally staggered to his feet.

"I'll be back when I'm not drunk, and you'll be sorry," he promised, his words slurred by either the alcohol, the beating or both.

I hadn't realized he was drunk when I knocked him out, but it didn't matter as Spinks was only noisy and would never have done anything to him. I soothed my shaken dog and went back into the house.

The next day, there was an angry knock on my front door. I was surprised to find the same guy who had attacked Spinks...and who I had knocked senseless. He menacingly narrowed his eyes and growled, "I'm sober now, asshole. Let's see how tough you are when I'm not drunk."

In a split second, I remembered some advice Ralph gave me—probably the only advice from him I'd ever listened to: *Always get the first punch in.* I also flashed back to the older bully and my successful first-strike attack on him. So, I channeled Bruce Lee and hammered the guy dead on the nose before he could blink. He hit the ground like a sack of dirt, out like a light. I waited for him to come to and then helped him up. As I've mentioned, in chess the pre-emptive strike has shock value, gives you control and allows you to set the tone of the game. It also puts your opponent on the defensive. However, in real life, as opposed to chess, you don't have to wait for the other guy to take his turn before striking again. Had the first punch not worked I wasn't going to wait and see what happened. I was going to keep hitting him until he went down. Turns out, it wasn't necessary. My first punch check-mated him.

Clearly embarrassed and taken aback, he smeared off the blood from his nose and sputtered he would have to burn my house down now. I kept my voice low and even and calmly talked him down from setting fire to my place. After all, I was barely into the mortgage. I was trying to recall if I even had fire insurance as I sold him on the idea of a truce. Jimmy, it turns out, would refrain from torching my house and actually become my friend. Perhaps, in the culture of the street, like the rest of the animal kingdom, by demonstrating my physical superiority and establishing the pecking order, it caused Jimmy to have to respect me. That grudging respect would eventually become a true friendship when he got to know me, and we began to discover things in common.

Charm City meets *On the Origin of Species*.

Even though we were adults, all the young neighborhood men played stickball just like kids in the 'hood over by the warehouses on Light Street. I was six-feet, one-ninety and could handle myself, a fact Jimmy discovered the hard way but eventually found comfort, as I was now his friend. In our neighborhood, the rule was a bit primal, and yes, a little bit Jack London-ish, in that the fittest survived and a devastating left hook spoke volumes about you. I wasn't a bad ass, just a man who wasn't going to take any shit. From anyone. I didn't get in too many fights as an adult. I don't know if it was because of my size or just projecting a vibe of dangerous confidence that let anyone know I was unafraid to throw down when confronted. Maybe I'd watched Sandy too much but one thing I'd learned being around that brute was that nobody but *nobody* fucked with Sandy.

It's human nature for aggressors to beat up opponents they know they can easily defeat. Just as in chess, it is key to make your opponent understand quickly by your actions that, while they just might win, the fight will be anything but easy, and they will have to pay a high price—whether a broken nose, a gouged eye, a loss of important pieces (including body parts) or a weakening of position—for their victory. This attitude served me well over the years. Of course, it didn't hurt to have Granddaddy Noonan's hot blood coursing through my veins either and a bipolar take-no-prisoners temperament. *Fight me, and I will give you something to remember me by* was how I both lived and played chess.

***

While my home life was stressful, at least I had the stable rhythms of work as a counterpoint. At Gunther's, I kept my head down, worked hard and smart and eventually clawed my way up from the shipping department to being one of the six salesmen on the front counter, a real leap. The position had some authority within the company and certainly paid better. It took a while but, as time passed in that sales position, my bosses saw my abilities and work ethic and, one day, made me head of the residential department. It was a huge promotion, as I did all the purchasing for everything except industrial supplies. On top of the considerable new responsibilities, they also gave me my own office, a generous space that looked down on the front sales counter.

As the residential buyer, I met the major builders, designers and architects of Baltimore as they built homes for wealthy clients, helping them select everything from door hardware to bath accessories. I became an expert in restoration hardware for historic buildings, and, with Baltimore's long and storied history, there were plenty of them.

I was very fortunate to be mentored by Roland "Eddie" Slaysman, perhaps the best door hardware expert in the country. When Eddie retired, I took his place and would eventually be recognized as one of the foremost experts in residential door hardware in the United States. And, yet, as success upon success piled up at Gunther's and my opinion began to carry more and more weight, having become a respected authority in my field, it just wasn't enough for my bipolar proclivities. No matter what I did, no matter what triumphs I experienced in chess or at work, that bipolar devil was always around, whispering occasionally in my ear that all was lost.

What's the point, Troy?

Despite my embarrassment of riches, I would at times feel the walls closing in and pushing out reality, imposing a dark, hopeless movie in my head that left me hollow and wanting out.

I attempted suicide again. This time I tied a rope around my neck and looped it over the cross bar that held the coats and jackets in the foyer closet. Perhaps I'd gotten the idea from my first meeting with Lucy when she described how her father had hung himself in the closet in the entry to their home. I tried a few configurations of the rope and the noose around my neck, but each time I put pressure on it, the rope came loose. Finally, I just said, "Fuck it," and abandoned my attempt to take my life, as I was too unmotivated to tighten the rope properly and make a successful go at it. I was also irritated that, as a hardware man, I should have been able to pull off a simple hanging. I decided to live as punishment for my incompetence.

Bipolar disorder can cause reckless behavior, sometimes insanely reckless behavior. Sometimes, it's just self-destructive, sometimes it's very risky, but you become like Mel Gibson's character, Martin Riggs, in the first *Lethal Weapon*: you know it's risky, maybe even fatal, and, yet, you persist because you really don't give a shit. It's like your instinct for self preservation just gets shut off like a switch. I found myself feeling bored over work, over life, over everything. I needed some action to kick start my adrenal glands, get my heart rate up. I felt like a combat veteran playing a stupid kid's video game. I needed the real fucking thing. I needed danger.

It came my way in the form of two Albert Gunther employees. The first was Herb. A stout man in his early fifties with a barrel chest and massive forearms, like Popeye, Herb worked the Will Call counter where customers would pick up the orders they called in. A real "feminist," Herb had a not infirm conviction that every woman had their price for sex. He first proved the Herb Theorem of Sex for Cash at Gunther's by negotiating a tryst with one of the cleaning ladies, a very well-endowed black woman.

Apparently, his success with the janitorial staff emboldened him to seek more company with black women. He told me the story of picking up a prostitute on North Avenue one Sunday soon after the first event. He made the deal with the hooker, she got in his car, and they drove a short distance away from the major thoroughfare and pulled over in front of a church to do their deed. Then, they got in the back seat, and he proceeded to fuck her from behind.

The church let out during their carnal act, and two black ladies in huge hats and resplendent in their Sunday best strolled by the car. One exclaimed loudly and with some umbrage as they passed, "Did you see that white boy fucking that girl, up the ass?"

Herb admitted he didn't know if their outrage was over the inter-racial nature of the sight or the fact it was happening in front of their church. Or both. Either way he was amused.

One time, Herb pulled over to negotiate a sexual encounter with a young black crackhead.

She asked, negotiating from a slightly drugged haze, "What's you want, sugah?"

Herb answered, "I'd like to go 'round the world.'" This was street slang for sampling *all* of her bodily openings.

She didn't hesitate. "That's gonna cost ya!"

"How much?"

"'S'gonna cost you every bit o' two oh," she slurred.

For a moment. Herb thought two hundred dollars was outrageous and balked until he came to his senses, remembered where he was and understood her to mean she was only talking about *two-oh*—twenty bucks, not two hundred. He was quite proud that he managed a world tour for such a bargain basement price. A cruise line would have charged a fortune.

Aside from his allocations of cash for sex, Herb also set aside a chunk of his pay each week to go to the track on Saturdays. Herb was quite the handicapper and actually won more often than he lost, something most people cannot claim. I was impressed with his percentage of wins and assumed I could do just as well, since I deemed Herb not to be anywhere close to being considered for membership in Mensa. I also proudly acknowledged the family history of investing in the outcome of two-minute equine contests, figuring it was in my blood, and started going to the track, like Herb.

I thought it would be a piece of cake, but, as it turned out, I was far less adept at handicapping horse racing and seemed to always lose. The last straw was when I only had two bucks to my name, and could not play a $4.00 exacta box on the 7 and 11 horses. For those less practiced at losing their money in such contests, the exacta requires the bettor to pick the winning and placing horses, i.e., first and second, in that order. Higher odds horses who land in this category of bet can pay off quite handsomely, as you'll see. I didn't have the extra two bucks to box the wager, in other words, bet 11 and 7—that is, reverse the order—so I placed the bet on the 7-11 Exacta only not boxed.

Of course, the race came in with the eleven and seven horses—winning and placing in that order, essential to the concept of the Exacta— and paid over six-hundred dollars for that two-buck wager...the one I *didn't* make because I chose its opposite. I was beside myself over such a ridiculous near miss and gave up horse racing, especially after suffering the indignity of having to walk seven miles home because I couldn't afford a cab. I was a flat, fucking broke loser. It felt like a sign of some kind. I decided I was done with gambling, period. Finito.

Or so I thought.

***

As fate would have it, my taste for gambling began anew when I met Mickey, another Gunther employee and yet another bad role model from whom to drink from his well of mis-experience. Mickey was a burly Canadian ex-hockey player who stood at least 6'4" with a wide-mouthed grin of missing teeth to prove his bona fides as a man who seemed to more often select fists over diplomacy. Mickey worked in the shipping department and was quite the sports betting enthusiast. He was so good at picking winners on football games, he earned the nickname, "Mick the Pick."

Despite his history of solving issues with violence, he was actually a good-natured lug who called every male "Big Guy." It sure seemed like a good way not to have to remember anyone's name.

One day he approached me and grandly stated, "Big Guy, I'm gonna make you a very happy man. Bet with me this week on the Colts-Patriots game. The Pats are giving 6 but will win by at least 14."

He seemed so sure of the bet and had that golden reputation, I handed over my entire pay check to bet on the game. The worst possible thing happened. We won, and, with that spark to the pile of tinder-dry refuse—also called my inability to control my emotions—there was no turning back for me. I was all in as a gambler again, despite the recent and very long walk home from the horse track with my empty pockets.

I bet with Mick the Pick every game he handicapped. During that football season, I won over fifteen thousand bucks which was a working man's fortune at the time. Unfortunately, football season ended, and the only real action—and fuel for my new addiction—was to bet basketball. Sadly, in the yin and yang of wagering, as good as Mick the Pick was at betting football, he was equally as bad at betting roundball.

Assuming your football prediction skills could be translated to basketball is like saying, I'm good at Mahjong, so I'll be good at chess. Both are complex, have lots of moving parts and require specific strategies but are from different planets. A little old lady flipping a coin could have crushed Mick's picks in the modern version of Dr. Naismith's invention.

Before the basketball season had even ended, we had returned all of our football bounty to the Gods of Gambling, given our catastrophic skills at picking "winners" on basketball games. I recall—very painfully, even now—he picked 16 straight losers at one point. I'd give you any odds that you could not lose that unequivocally. The final straw for me came in the spring of 1982 when we bet several thousand dollars—*which we did not have*—on the Washington Bullets and six points against the Boston Celtics laying the six.

The Bullets were up by three points with seconds to play in the game. Mick and I were celebrating and hugging each other since that we had the six-point spread and a three-point lead, so there was no chance to lose.

Oh, but there was.

With absolutely no time on the clock, save for some unit of measure maybe a physicist could argue, shooting guard Danny Ainge hit a three-pointer to take the game into overtime. Mick and I sat down, stunned, the wind knocked out of us. In that cold, cruel, unsympathetic instant, we both knew we were going to lose. And we did. Celtics won by nine in overtime. And I lost a ton of money I did not have.

I had to go to my Grandmother Noonan, hat in hand, with grave shame to borrow the money to pay off the debt. She knew the world her daughter—my mother—had been living for years, and she knew you didn't cross those people when you owed them. She handed over that cash to make me whole, and it took me two years to pay her back, but I finally did. Acknowledging my limitations, as any chess player must do, I gave up sports betting for good.

***

Although I had a great job, was admired and respected for my knowledge of my field and had finally let go of my destructive gambling impulses, I was still not happy. My undiagnosed bipolar condition caused me to endure a roller coaster ride of depression, followed by intense mania for weeks at a time. Then, like a hurricane passing, I'd enter the eye of my disorder and things seemed almost normal. For a while. Without having had a professional tell me what was really wrong with me, I just chalked it up to being extremely moody. Moodiness was sort of the blanket prevailing opinion back then regarding bipolar sufferers.

I admitted to myself I was bored with Lucy and bored living in South Baltimore among people with room temperature IQs. I longed to be back at Uncle Jake's in Mount Vernon where there was much more culture and diversity. I fantasized about chucking it all and running away to New York. This was just part of the reckless fantasizing that was part of the reckless behavior that draws many people with bipolar. Danger is our middle name. I visualized myself becoming a professional chess player and the hell with everything else. Then, reason would prevail. I still wanted to be anywhere but South Baltimore, but I felt anchored, obligated. I just couldn't seem to light the fuse to blow it all up.

Then, one evening, Lucy and I had a huge fight. I don't even remember what it was about, but, in a fit of rage, Lucy went over to the bookshelf where I kept my chess books and, in a move calculated to inflict maximum emotional injury on me, proceeded to hurl them down off the shelves. This act of defilement was the final straw, abusing my chess books. I snapped. I gathered my books off the floor, threw together a suitcase full of clothes and personal items and headed off to the safe haven of Uncle Jake's. I left Lucy the house and the car and took only what I could carry and never looked back. We divorced a year later.

***

Despite getting out of my stultifying existence with Lucy in the sticks of South Baltimore, I still had some moments of stress. One day, I was enjoying a normal day at Gunther's, when I had a frightful experience that left me shaken and confused. Willy was a black man with bouts of mania. He had served time in prison, but with his debt paid, he was given a job at Gunther's and eventually worked his way up to running the shipping department. That day, his men and he were tossing boxes of locksets down a flight of stairs to save themselves the few steps it would take to carry them down.

I had bought every one of those locksets and knew many were valuable and almost all were vulnerable to having their finishes scratched or damaged. I watched this lazy process for a moment and got angry.

"Hey," I yelled at Willy. "Quit throwing those locksets! Carry 'em downstairs! You're gonna damage 'em!"

He was furious and quietly followed me down the stairs until I was in a secluded space in the basement. Then, he pounced and grabbed my shirt, shoving me against the wall, putting a knife to my throat, all so fast I had no time to react.

"I'mna kill you motherfucker for talkin' to me like that!"

What I did next completely threw my would-be killer. I relaxed in his grip and lowered my arms.

"Willy, you'd be doing me a fuckin' favor. I didn't have the guts to kill myself the other day, but now you can do it for me. Go for it. Please, I'm fucking begging you."

Willy stared at me wide-eyed for a moment, unsure of what he'd just heard. Then he did something I never would have seen coming in a million years. His expression changed completely, his dark eyes welled with tears, and he pressed me into a bear hug as he broke down and wept without any shame.

"Hey, man," he said, through his tears, "I'm sorry. I'm real sorry man. I love you, brother. I'm so sorry."

He kissed me on the cheek. "I love you, brother."

I hugged him back, and, from that moment on, we were friends.

***

After leaving Lucy, I was forced to move into Uncle Jake and Aunt Peggy's apartment building despite Uncle Jake having a full house of tenants at the time. Nevertheless, he found me a room and soon it was just like old times, except without Uncle Jake's colorful crew hanging around. Despite having become one of his detested lunch bag men, Uncle Jake was genuinely proud of what I had become and what I'd accomplished at Gunther's. I also noticed he never railed about lunch bag men any more, at least not when I was around.

After work, I would go over to the Mount Vernon Tavern on Mount Royal Avenue. I drank rum and cokes and hustled chess. The Mount Vernon Tavern was frequented by art students from the Maryland Institute of Art and a collection of artists who had graduated from the Institute but apparently liked the vibe and stayed in Baltimore. I loved the Tavern because I was among poets and artists who all treated me as a fellow artist because I was a chess Master. They considered playing chess a skill they considered a form of art, and it commanded a lot of respect from them. It was nice validation from people I respected and, admittedly, a breath of fresh intellectual air in which to steep myself from the people I spent most of my days and nights around.

CHAPTER TEN

Improving My Performance Rating in Life

"The pupil wants not so much to learn, as to learn how to learn."
—Samuel Boden, English Chess Master

I trounced everyone who dared play me for money, and, when I was not hustling chess, I would play a fiendish game of Pac Man on machines at the bar. Yeah, it was that long ago.

One night, a petite woman of around thirty came into the Mount Vernon Tavern and sat at the bar, near the booth where I was hustling chess. She watched intently as I made my moves, almost instantaneously against an opponent who labored over his moves. She had mesmerizing blue eyes and long, blondish hair. She was an unconventional beauty, a younger version of Margaret Hamilton, the actress who played the Wicked Witch of the West in *The Wizard of Oz*. And she had a way of carrying herself and a sexy confidence that had me absolutely taken by her. Her name was Elizabeth, and, to me, she was stunning. Others would simply say, *"Yeah, she's nice...but doesn't she look a little like Margaret Hamilton...only younger."*

Maybe, but I didn't care. I liked Margaret Hamilton, and I liked Elizabeth.

She seemed to be sort of a regular and, as time went by, I wanted to get to know her better. The first time I asked her out, she turned me down, flat. I was a bit surprised, but her denial gave me even more motivation. I didn't like losing, and I was intrigued. She was complicated, so I had to see what made her tick. I saw her a few more times at the tavern, and, each time, I asked her out again, and she politely, but firmly, refused to go out with me. Finally, I'd had enough of the abuse and confronted her. I felt we seemed to have something in common, I wasn't a bad guy, and I thought we might have fun. I could see no good reasons for her rejection.

I came out and said it. "So, how come you keep declining my offers for dates? I'm a nice guy. A good chess player and have a good job. I'm not trying to overthrow the government, and I've never robbed a bank. So, what's the problem?"

I was hoping a little humor might loosen her up. I knew she was very smart. We were alone in a booth, and so she apparently decided she could be brutally honest as to why she would not date me.

"First," she began her lecture, almost as if she'd practiced giving it, "you wear polyester pants and shirts. Unacceptable. Secondly, your speech is that of a person of the lower class, despite your obvious intellect. You're a really smart man, yet you speak as if you work on the docks. Third, and I'm doing you a favor telling you this, but you're fat."

I was a bit stunned. Sure, I was a little overweight, being, well, over two hundred pounds at the time...okay, probably quite a few pounds over my "fighting weight," but I'd never considered myself any Fatty Arbuckle. I was crushed and pissed, all at the same time. My jaw went slack, and I got up and walked away, my tail between my legs. I went home in a daze. Now I wanted her even more, since I couldn't have her, let alone the fact she thought I was a fat-assed, polyester-wearing gutter-trash piece of shit....oh, who also played chess. Goddammit, I'd show her. I'd *have* her one day, and that was that.

I did some digging and found out Elizabeth was from an old, wealthy Baltimore family with a lineage of doctors. Her grandfather was a famous doctor whose name was chiseled into a plaque in one of the Johns Hopkins Hospital buildings.

When I confronted her again, I asked her, "How you like your men to dress?"

She didn't hesitate, replying quickly and crisply. "Simply. Clean, white Oxford shirts, one hundred percent cotton, and if it gets hot you may roll up the sleeves, but never wear short-sleeve shirts. One hundred percent cotton, blue jeans and black leather loafers, hopefully a decent brand, and of course, with no socks."

Of course. Huh? What the hell did she have against socks?

Now I was intrigued. She'd obviously put a lot of thought into her comments.

Perhaps too much. But if it should have been seen as a red flag, my perception was that of a bull. It just drew me in more.

I continued. "So how does my speech offend you?"

She shook her head like a school marm. "You sound like Huntz Hall from the Bowery Boys. You say yous instead of you, and you savagely butcher English, in general. Did you go to school in the United States of America? Because, if you did, I'd request a refund."

Her staggeringly impertinent question and snipe left me reeling, belittled and even more determined to win her over. I felt like the guy, Jimmy, who beat my poor dog Spinks, then had me hand him his hat several times with my fists. Only Elizabeth's words hurt a helluva lot more than my punches did. It was like I was in the presence of some fiendish Henry Higgins, the fictional professor of phonetics in *My Fair Lady* who bets that he can teach Cockney flower girl Eliza Doolittle how to speak proper English. I somehow had to please her and climb the slopes to her approval. What next? Marbles in my mouth as I recite Proust?

I rushed home and threw out every article of clothing with even a hint of polyester. The next day after work, I went on an upgrading shopping spree, buying several white Oxford shirts, along with the prescribed blue jeans and black leather loafers. I bought absolutely no socks. I researched and read books on speaking proper English, books on how to win a woman and books on how to make love to a woman. I felt like I was gearing up for the biggest job interview of my life. I began transforming myself into a preppie god.

I was terribly out of practice at sex because I had only slept with Lucy, and that had been some time before. And Lucy was hardly demanding in bed given her only sex had really been with me and being raped. Yes, it was very sad but having a partner with such limitations left me limited as well. I felt if I got that far Elizabeth would be as schooled and as demanding in that respect as she was with matters sartorial, so I'd damn well better be ready.

I stopped drinking alcohol and anything else with empty calories or too many carbs. To that end, I cut out all sugar and starches. The pounds started to drop off immediately. In two months, I was down to a cut one-seventy-three. I went from a size forty waistline to a thirty-four. I was reglazed in the kiln of self-improvement and was now ready to go after Elizabeth with the same energy, devotion and dedication I had gone after chess. I had reinvented myself like Robert De Niro did for *Raging Bull* (only the opposite direction), or better, like Rocky did to fight Apollo. I was ready to take the title.

How far was I willing to go, other than completely replacing Troy1.1 with Troy1.2? I opened the Mount Royal Chess Club at the corner of Calvert Street and Mount Royal Avenue just to impress Elizabeth. Of course, I kept my job at Gunther's Hardware so the added duty of now having a club to run after work put extra pressure on me. But extra pressure for anyone with bipolar disorder can destroy them or give them extraordinary power, like that Japanese movie monster who eats power... whatever his name.

To furnish the club, we "borrowed" the tables and chairs from the Mount Royal Hotel across the street that had closed several years earlier. As I made my way in the pitch dark to the grand ballroom of the old hotel, it was like visiting the Titanic. I snuck the tables and chairs out through the fire escapes. I saved hundreds of dollars by swiping my furnishings from that old inn.

Of course, being the highbrow, Elizabeth hung with a literary crowd and her favorite writer was poet Andrei Codrescu, a Romanian who wrote a weekly column for one of Baltimore's newspapers. She had met Codrescu once and was mesmerized by his intelligence and Romanian charm. By a stroke of luck, the Mount Royal Chess Club happened to be next door to a house full of poets. Many of these poets were disciples of German-born Charles Bukowski, the hard-drinking California poet who embraced America's urban underbelly. The poets emulated his writing style and tried to copy him as best they could. I started to hang with the poets. I also started reading Charles Bukowski.

I know my obsessive program to remake myself did not go unnoticed by Elizabeth. As the weeks went by and the pounds came off, she also saw how my wardrobe had evolved from rough-around-the-edges, blue-collar exec to slick prepster and how I'd made a big effort to sound more like Alistair Cooke and less Leo Durocher. I could feel her warming up to me finally. While the attraction had been there, I think to her I was like a fixer-upper that a guy sees and figures that, with some engine work, a new paint job and a full interior detail, he'd be proud to drive to his high school reunion. Knowing that, I still didn't mind.

To further impress Elizabeth, I invited her to a bar in Fells Point that had an open mic night for poets. I read from the stage the one and only poem I had ever written, about 1315 North Calvert Street. I recited it, looking directly at Elizabeth.

Here it is:

1315

The man in Apartment C makes obscene calls,
Heard through plaster walls,
Threatening women with a tongue not used for their pleasure.
The drunken nympho brings home a stranger—

She will walk with pain in the morning.
A young waitress rents the second-floor rear apartment
Knows not that fumigation can hide a closet grave.
The old bookie with yellow beard and nails
Quietly charting his stocks—never bought
From his tiny room these twenty years passed
He's out performed Legg Mason.
I sit in the dark of my third-floor room, windows open
Feeling the summer swell…
Listening to the hum of Waverly Press.
As I gaze down at the alleys below,
Reflecting on the path of life
That has brought me back again to thirteen-fifteen.
—Troy Roberts, 1983

I hoped Mr. Bukowski, the godfather of "dirty realism," would have liked it and shared a drink (or ten) with me. Maybe he would have liked it so much we would have gotten in a fight and that would have been cool, too, since we'd be alive. The poem was a hit at the bar and, more importantly, with Elizabeth. I was proud I had managed to get that pawn to the back row and achieve my goal. I went home with Elizabeth that night to her apartment on Cathedral Street, and we made love for hours.

I never had experienced sex like that night. It was magical and opened a door to experiences that I had never accurately imagined though I'd tried. Kind of like you can see pictures of the Grand Canyon, but you have to stand on its edge to believe it. Elizabeth warned me she had contracted herpes in college. I didn't care. I would not wear a rubber, and I was very anxious to taste a woman since I had never gone down on Lucy. Like studying chess, the sex techniques I had learned from books worked. I could make Elizabeth climax time and time again. It was then I realized that Lucy had never had an orgasm with me, as I was a poor lover back then. While I had no luck with basketball or horses, I lucked out with Elizabeth and never contracted herpes.

***

My long-term strategy and carefully-plotted moves paid off. I moved in with Elizabeth a month or so later. But all of the perfect white shirts and loafers and broadcast English diction couldn't help when it came to the disruptive force of my bipolar moods. This issue made things increasingly difficult for us. While she'd seen and addressed the items on her agenda that she could see—the aforementioned, that is—she didn't really know my "quirks" until we became intimate and began to live together, so the sinister secrets that lay between my ears and in the dark recesses of my brain and behavior had not made it onto her "to-do" list.

The other thing was that Elizabeth's project to "polish me up" turned out to be more successful than she'd planned or expected. There were unforeseen complications to the transformation she'd been instrumental in bringing about. While I was much more attractive to her, I was also attractive to other women. I took advantage of my new-found celebrity. After so long with one deeply repressed sexual partner—Lucy—I was like a newly wealthy kid who just learned to drive, decided he really liked cars and suddenly had the wherewithal to try a lot of fun cars. In that case, the analogous money was my new attractiveness and sexual desires, as fed by my bipolar libido, which pushed me to start fucking around with other women. A lot of other women. Take a kid to a car lot filled with Jaguars and Porsches and Corvettes, tell him he has carte blanche, and he'll want to take each one for a ride.

Many with bipolar are promiscuous and engage in extremely risky behavior, especially sexual behavior. Seeking and having many partners was almost a reflex. I didn't really think about the women, other than how they excited me and how they helped fulfill my rapacious sexual drive. While I had Elizabeth at home, she just wasn't enough, particularly with the newly-discovered cachet I had with many women. They all seemed to want me, and I wanted them. I was in hog heaven and did what I pleased and made sure Elizabeth had no idea I was dipping my wick all over the place.

At Gunther's, one of my duties was working with designers and their clients while they built or renovated their homes. Most of the designer's clients were rich, bored housewives whose husbands were too busy making money at their businesses or practices and, on top of that, probably fucking around with their own mistresses. These neglected socialites were looking for fun and were low-hanging fruit for affairs. There were times I was juggling two or three hot cougars at the same time. It was not easy, and it was dangerous, as many of the husbands were extremely powerful movers and shakers in Baltimore. Had any of these men of stature in the community discovered some schlub at the building supply was tapping their trophy wives, I would have had to find new employment at another building supply. Probably in Nome. If I was lucky.

As for my "conquests," while I assume many men would be overjoyed to be engaging in such relentless sexual liaisons, I can assure you it was a living hell. It was stress inducing, juggling so many women and then coming home to Elizabeth. I hoped none of them would ever trade notes with the others or that somehow Elizabeth would find out about my affairs through her society grapevine. How I got away with it, God only knows. I suppose it was a combination of luck and smarts, but likely a lot more of the former. It got to be a nail-biting strain, and, then, one day, some of my sexual empire came crashing down.

While I'd dodged the herpes bullet, I was not so lucky with gonorrhea. When I brought it home to Elizabeth, she threw me out in a fit of rage. Now, I was back at Uncle Jake's and the eternal North Calvert Street. The collapse of my relationship with Elizabeth caused me to reflect on whether I was a horrible person and, perhaps, even a sociopath. This line of thinking continued for a long time, and, over the years, it presented itself from time to time during periods of stress and made me wonder why I did what I did. I would chalk it up as a character flaw and then work hard to bury it in my conscience until it popped back again. It was only years later, when working with Marsha, my therapist, did she make me come to the realization that my bipolar condition was the impetuous for such reckless and abhorrent behavior. Was it an excuse? I chose not to see it that way but, rather, as a reason, not just some gaping hole in my integrity.

***

While my personal and sexual life was often chaotic, my chess club was thriving, and I seemed to draw a wildly eclectic crowd. The club provided me with great intellectual stimulation as the people drawn to chess are generally pretty bright, regardless of their background, whether cultured or street. I began giving lessons to an economics professor at Johns Hopkins University named Hugh Rose, and we became good friends. In addition to Hugh and a few academics, the club featured a cast of eccentric characters and a large number of African-American chess players, some of them quite gifted.

Expert chess player Dino Pete literally spoke only two words, regardless of the question or statement.

"Say whaaaaat?" was his answer to everything.

You could say, "Hi Dino," and he would respond, "Say whaaaaat?"

It didn't matter what you said. "Do you want to play a game of chess?" or "Hey Dino, did you hear the earth is about to be destroyed by a rogue asteroid?" would elicit the same "Say whaaaaat?" His responses might have been limited but his game was not.

There was Stroke, a light-skinned black chess hustler. Legend had it that Stroke got his nickname when he once played a chess move so unexpected and shocking it apparently stunned his opponent into falling out of his chair and dying of a stroke on the spot, a tactic never mentioned in any of the myriad chess books I've read.

Top that, Fischer!

William "The Exterminator" Morrison was a young, stick-thin, black chess hustler from New York who was so strong he could use only three minutes to my five on the chess clock and still clobber me. I remember his eyes were like lasers when he locked your gaze.

Baby Z was another player who patterned his game after the great Russian chess player Roman Dzindzichashvili, hence his nickname. But Baby Z's game was nowhere near Grandmaster Roman's game, so everyone wanted to play Baby Z and transfer the cash from his wallet to theirs.

The black players called me Ghostbuster and would hum the theme of the movie *Ghostbusters* when I would enter the club. They called me Ghostbuster because I would play anyone for money and "he ain't afraid o' no ghosts."

One night, a black chess player with a big mustache and movie star good looks came to town from Chicago. His name was Emory Tate, and he went on to become an International Master. Emory spoke fluent German, Spanish and Russian and had done a stint in the Air Force. All the African-American players were exceedingly proud of him, because he was one of the strongest black players in the country. He was sort of the Michael Jordan of chess, and they were eager to set up a five-minute blitz match between us.

I accepted his challenge and was given the singular experience of understanding how General Custer felt. He massacred me 24-0. I was never so humiliated in my life. I was stunned. All the black players reveled in his victory. *"Ghostbuster got busted!"*

Several weeks later, in a major rated tournament at Johns Hopkins University, I had another chance at recovering my honor—or getting killed again—when I played Emory for the first-place prize money. This time, when it really counted, I beat The Man, when he played the Dutch Defense. The Dutch is a very aggressive opening and unbalances your kingside, while contributing nothing to your development. It can, however, have a destabilizing effect on your opponent if they don't immediately address it. But, if your adversary sees through you,

you can be in grave danger. It's rarely used at such a high level but has been known to happen...and work. Fortunately, I read his deceit like a building-sized electric billboard on the Ginza and quickly had him on the run. The truth was he was crushed right out of the opening because he underestimated me. I made sure everyone heard about my victory. Sadly, Emory left us several years ago at the too-young age of 56. But he went out in the saddle, collapsing in the middle of a chess tournament.

***

Of all the colorful characters at my club, at the top of the list of the most offbeat, would without a doubt be Give-a-Fuck, a dangerous and notorious drug dealer who loved him some chess. Unfortunately for Mr. Fuck, he was not very good at it. Everyone played him for money and would win, but Give-a-Fuck didn't give a shit because his drug sales revenue was considerable. He was Superfly with a Jones for the most mind-testing board game ever invented and financed his addiction through other's addictions. It was both wonderfully ironic and lucrative.

One night, Give-a-Fuck challenged me to spot him five minutes for one of my minutes on the chess clock. The wager? One crisp Benjamin Franklin a game. Or, in his case, probably a well-rolled Mr. Franklin with some white residue on the edges, but either way they all spent the same. Figuring it was at least an easy hundred bucks, I accepted his challenge.

It turned out to be a little more than a hundred.

Like ten thousand. He kept pulling hundred dollar bills out of his sweatsuit, game after game, losing every time, then upping the ante. He may not have been a good chess player, but he was very competitive. Finally, he'd exhausted the bankroll in his pockets and asked that we keep playing, but on credit. Being tired, as well as ecstatic I had won so much money, I turned him down, wanting to take a rest and enjoy my money. Plus, I felt more than a twinge of guilt for having taken him to the cleaners, despite his being a willing participant.

To let him off the hook, I suggested, "Let's pick up the games when you've got more money next time."

Give-a-Fuck's face twisted in rage as he went ballistic and screamed at me, "You muthafuckin' Jew bastard!! You fuckin' cheap Jew bastard!! You coulda had ten times what you won tonight, but you were too fuckin' cheap!!"

Then, to emphasize his point, he grabbed me and pulled me out to his car and opened the trunk. Taking up most of the trunk were two large duffle bags stuffed to the brim. It would have been a considerable amount of laundry, but, in fact, they contained enough folding money to make envious Tony Montana, the main fictional protagonist of the mafia film "Scarface."

He continued to rage at me. "You cheap motherfuckin' Jew bastard, you coulda had all this but you were too fuckin' cheap!!"

Then, he slammed the trunk and drove away, still fuming. While Give-a-Fuck's tantrum and sacks of dough gave me pause, I did not engage in any what-ifs and went back into the club, more rattled by his fury than by my possible massive loss. Fuck it, I had ten grand, and that's all that mattered. Had I taken the poor bastard to the cleaners for some absurd sum, I would have felt bad. It was like beating up some preschooler.

Nevertheless, the ten thousand bucks was no chump change, and with it I realized I now had the ability to implement some big changes. I made the decision to quit Gunther, give up my chess club and move to New York City. I had met this zaftig Irish girl named Molly at the tavern. Molly had black, bang-cut hair, ala Cleopatra. She probably weighed around what I did, but it didn't matter to me. Despite her heft she was kind of cute and had an edge I valued at the time. She dressed in all-black and was sort of a faux Goth because she came from a wealthy family in Cleveland. She enjoyed posing as an alt and kept quiet from her fellow Bohemians that she had just graduated from Goucher College, which at that time was a private women's college north of Baltimore.

Two interesting things about Goucher College: they have the highest Jewish population of any U.S. school and, unlike any other college in this country, require students to spend time studying abroad. I thought it was a good idea to ask Molly if she wanted to move up to New York with me. She was very intelligent and extremely funny, and she opened doors to worlds I did not know. She turned me on to music that I had never experienced: Echo and the Bunny Men, The Psychedelic Furs, New Order, The Smiths and the Cure.

She also built up my ego when she paid me a rather extraordinary compliment by remarking I had a particularly large body part.

"You are well-hung," she said, matter-of-factly. What guy doesn't want to hear that? Molly loved to fuck, and I enjoyed that quality.

Once we agreed to set off for New York and had plans fairly solidified,

I gave notice at Gunther. They tried hard to make me stay, but I was determined to go up to New York and test myself against the best chess players in the country. I sold the chess club for a thousand bucks to a black chess player named Skylar. Then, Molly and I moved into a one-bedroom apartment on the Upper West Side of Manhattan, right on Riverside Drive near 86th Street. Our rent was eleven hundred a month.

As we were moving our belongings into the apartment, I thought of Frank Sinatra and his contention that if you could make it here you could make it anywhere. I was about to find out.

***

Moving to New York made me manic in a way I had never felt before. I felt charged, electrified. Every sensory feeling I had was operating at maximum. Smell, taste, hearing touch. My mind exploded with this neural overload and feelings of near invincibility. I felt I could do anything. I was brought to life in the city that never sleeps in a way that I'd never before experienced. I loved drinking in the smells of New York, the sweet aroma of dough and cheese blending from the pizza parlors, the scent of car and bus exhausts on the streets, the cologne and body odor and piss stench of the subways. They were all a symphony of olfactory overloads. I loved the salty, musty breeze that came off the Hudson while I was playing chess in Washington Square Park.

I was going a million miles-an-hour setting up a life in New York City.

I know it's such a cliché, as countless people before me and after me have chased their dreams in New York, but I felt I had finally made it. I was living the dream in New York City, and I was about to find out if Old Blue Eyes was right.

***

While I still had some of Give-A-Fuck's cash, I didn't want to fritter it away, so I wasted no time applying for a job at the premier decorative hardware showroom in New York City, Kraft Hardware. The owner, Stan Saperstein, hired me on the spot. My reputation and experience at Gunther's had turned me into a commodity. While Albert Gunther had been Baltimore's top building supply, going to Kraft and New York City was like moving up from AA ball to the Yankees. It was a whole new world, and I loved it. I became Stan's number one salesman within a month. My customers were the wealthiest of the wealthy, movie stars, music legends, the Masters of the Universe of Wall Street and the moguls who made the economy of New York and Manhattan—not to mention the world—tick.

My customers would eventually include Kathleen Turner, Billy Joel's designer, Yoko Ono, Liza Minnelli, Lauren Bacall and Brooke Shield's mother, Teri. The nicest, most memorable star I waited on was Sigourney Weaver, a beautiful and classy woman. She was the first person to show me the power of repeating someone's name to cement a connection and to gain power over someone.

Sigourney would say, "What do think of this, Troy?" or "What is best, Troy?" or "Can we try this, Troy?" I would never have disagreed with the woman who killed hulking acid-for-blood aliens like cockroaches, but I later realized the more she used my name the more she controlled me. Once I figured out her secret, I embraced the technique and used it to huge advantage later in life. Thanks, Sigourney.

New York City (the Russians might disagree) is the Mecca of chess, and I played in chess tournaments with the best players in the country. I would try and hustle chess in Washington Square Park in the Village, but, more often than not, I was the one who got hustled because the caliber of chess players in New York was off the charts.

Molly reinvented herself by ditching her Goth persona and made a one-eighty about-face to a Laura Ashley vibe. Her new found "civility" (and probably *approachability*) immediately landed her a job in advertising. We were living a fairly good life in Manhattan, but I still could not find happiness. It just eluded me. I could tick off the things that were going right and how I should be over the moon with happiness and contentment, but I felt sort of hollow inside. Like someone had gotten hold of the "joy" rheostat in my brain and potted it all the way down. I didn't know what was wrong with me, and it would be years before I would find out that this anchor of anxiety was caused by the bipolar monkey on my back.

Like a lot of people until they are diagnosed, I just chalked it up to some sort of character failing and lived with it. I'd get the urge to just bolt, chuck it all and head to California or some place where the grass seemed greener. On one level, I knew it was not rational, and yet I was never satisfied regardless of how successful I became. I was never content, ever. It was not Molly's fault, it was all mine. And, by that, I mean it was all thanks to my constant companion, bipolar disorder. The disease, which at that point in my life I didn't even know I had, let alone have a name to call.

CHAPTER ELEVEN

King, Meet the Queen

"When you see a good move, look for a better one."
—Emanuel Lasker, World Chess Champion

I was doing really well at Kraft, and both my job and New York agreed with me. Molly and I had a good relationship but it wasn't amazing, it was just that: good. While I wasn't unhappy with her, neither was I considering a life with her, a future together. She had been my companion on the journey out of Baltimore and now my partner in a place to live and the shared experience of the Big Apple, but that was it.

I arrived at work one morning and went to the front door to open the showroom for business and found a slim, gorgeous blonde with huge blue eyes and an elegant demeanor on the other side of the glass. She smiled at me as I approached, keys in hand, and I felt a twinge of electricity shoot down my back. Her name was Margaret, and to my joy I discovered she was not just a hot customer to flirt with for an hour but, rather, she was starting that day as a salesperson for the showroom. Smitten by her beauty, I happily volunteered to show her around the place. I asked Stan if I could train her and get her situated in her first week at Kraft.

After working with her for a few days, I could feel a playful spark developing between us and was very attracted to her. Despite the fact she was very friendly, laughed at my silly jokes and seemed to make a lot of eye contact, I still had no idea if the deepening feelings I had for her were mutual.

I didn't know it at the time, but other employees came up to her when they heard I was training her and would say things like, "Oh, you poor thing." Margaret good-naturedly nodded but wasn't sure what they meant. She would hear these sorts of hints from people that perhaps working with me was a problem. Margaret didn't understand, because she felt that I not only treated her well, but she liked me and saw no bad qualities. Finally, she gently confronted one of the rumor mongers about why she should be pitied for being put under my tutelage. She was hoping desperately there wouldn't be some deep, dark, awful secret about me.

"Oh," said the woman, "We all wonder how you keep up with him. He's so hyper. He moves like he's had ten cups of coffee!"

Margaret had to laugh. It was true she had to acknowledge my vigor, but Margaret had a level of energy herself that others found hard to keep up with, so we were a good fit. Margaret was deeply relieved the secret hadn't been that I was a suspected serial killer.

We worked on the sales floor together for about five months. Margaret eventually became the number two sales performer behind me. As time passed, my emotional response to anything concerning Margaret grew, and I found myself looking forward to work, much less about the excitement of new sales or customers, but more so about seeing her. Though I continued to do my job well, work became less about Kraft and more about where I would see Margaret.

One day, Margaret made a really strong hardware sale—I think it was around $5,000--that had been difficult to pull off, and I went right to our boss and bragged about how good she was. It seemed to me to be a no-brainer. She'd done really well, and I was proud of her. I didn't hear about this until years later but when Margaret found out that I'd reported her big sale—instead of trying to take credit myself or simply covering it up to steal her glory, situations she was more used to having

happen—she was quite touched, and that added mightily to her estima-
tion of me.

One weekend, Molly was going out to the Hamptons with some
college friends. I saw an opening and asked Margaret if she wanted to
go to dinner and then a movie or a comedy club while Molly was away.
Margaret turned me down and made it crystal clear she would never
go on a date with anyone who had a girlfriend. That was the moment I
knew I had to break it off with Molly and pursue Margaret.

It was a spur-of-the-moment decisiveness I'd developed as a chess
player. Don't get tied to an outcome if another, better one, presents
itself. In chess, you can usually see such things coming, since you're playing a number of moves ahead, unless, of course, you're playing another
Master. In life, shit happens, and you roll with it. Chess, and my chaotic
life to that point, taught me to have those life-changing decisions ready
to rock, locked and loaded, like torpedoes in their tubes. While leaving
Molly seemed like a snap of the fingers play, it wasn't. It just happened
to go down when Margaret made her move and presented me with her
assessment of reality. If I was to play her game, I needed to do so and do
it without regret.

Of course, my life game was never quite so sure as my chess game,
and in the back of my mind, a little voice said *you always want what you
can't have and are never satisfied with what you do have.* But I did my best
to ignore it. When Molly came back from the Hampton's, I gave her
the bad news and moved out of our apartment. I moved in with a chess
player friend who had an apartment in South Street Seaport on the very
southern tip of Manhattan.

With Margaret's dating caveat now moot because Molly was out of
the picture and no longer an issue, she agreed to go out with me. After a
few dates and some memorable moments, we both felt the heat between
us and finally made love and spent a romantic night at the St. Moritz.
It was a heady change of pace to make love to a woman who wasn't carrying a lot of extra pounds around. Margaret looked like a model. She
was the best-looking woman I'd been with, and that just increased my

desire for her. We also had great magnetism. While Margaret was a little reserved and quiet, I found it relaxing, particularly after Molly who was such a powerful and loud personality. Molly filled a room, which could be an advantage at a party or social event, but it could also get tiring.

Then, one night, after about three weeks of dating, Margaret looked me square in the eyes and blew my mind.

"I'm really tired of this dating thing. I'm looking to get married. Do you want to get married?"

Of course, I did, but her directness startled me...in a good way. Like I said, she was quiet, not mousy. Many good salespeople have big personalities and make up in bluster what they might lack in details or nuance. Margaret was a very good salesperson because she listened, had every detail possible at her command and had a strength of character that didn't require her to be the life of the party. She never made a lot of noise. She just pressed ahead without any drama, playing her low-key but strong, resolved game.

With Margaret's proposal, I had to reflect on the old expression that goes *What's not to like?* Margaret had assets. She owned her own apartment in Forest Hills, Queens, and had at least twenty thousand in the bank. Super-intelligent, she spoke three languages fluently. She was half-Italian, half-Hungarian. Her parents were an American success story, having come to America with practically nothing but, slowly and with great strength of character, managing to accrue a decent amount of wealth.

***

Her father Daniel's Jewish family owned a huge grain mill in Hungary and was extremely rich. After World War I, the portion of war-torn and politically-confused Hungary that would be Daniel's home became Yugoslavia. Weathering the persecution of Jews during that time, Daniel managed to study architecture in Zagreb. He was also a world-class fencer and ski jumper and made the Yugoslav Olympic teams in ski jumping and fencing for the 1936 Olympics. Unfortunately, the Jews on the teams (Daniel included) boycotted the 1936 Olympics in Germany because the host of the games, one Mr. Adolf Hitler, made the central theme a celebration of Aryan superiority. When the war broke out, despite his original Hungary siding with the Axis powers, Daniel was now a member of a different team and ideology and joined the Yugoslav army as a cavalry soldier.

When he was captured by the Germans, the hardest part of being captured was leaving his beloved horse tied to a tree, he told me. He never forgot the sad look on his horse's face as he was led away. Knowing the fate of Jews in Nazi hands, Daniel made a daring escape from his prison camp and swam naked across the Rhine River in the dead of winter. He knew that, if he was captured, he'd never make it back to the camp because the SS would put a bullet in his brain and leave his naked body in a ditch.

He miraculously managed to escape, but the terrible exposure and scrapes and cuts along the rocks caused him to lose all his fingernails and toenails. His luck was with him when a Quaker family found him and took him in. They nursed him back to health and, when he healed, sent him on his way to freedom.

He was one tough sonofabitch. In addition to Hungarian, Yugoslavian, Spanish and Italian, he spoke German fluently, since one of his nannies had been German when he was a child. Making his way out of Germany through Spain and Portugal, he made it to England and joined the RAF. He flew bombing missions over Africa, yet another miracle of survival since bomber crews had the highest rate of mortality in the war. Daniel got through it, but his losses beggared the imagination. His mother, father and brother, along with the rest of his immediate family, were all gone by way of the concentration camps of the Third Reich. His family was wiped out as was every penny of their wealth, all pumped into Hitler's war.

Margaret's mother, Giulia, came from a wealthy family in Rome and neither were they spared the icy hand of fate of World War. Her family owned a major taxi and trucking company, and, at first, life under the fascist dictator Mussolini was not too bad, but in 1936 the Italian army decided to confiscate all of her father's trucks and cabs and shipped them off to the Ethiopian War, leaving him broke. To add injury to insult, Giulia's father was then drafted into the army when she was twelve, and she didn't see him again for eight years. Her family managed to survive the war by selling off her mother's jewelry piece by piece for whatever scraps of food they could find.

Fortunately, Giulia's mother found a black-market merchant who sold a concoction of ground vegetable paste that could be used to make soup. Her family lived off that paste for four years. Margaret's mother, Giulia, was a beautiful and an emotionally complex woman. During the war, just as with Daniel's family, her family lost everything they had with the exception of their lives. Her father was missing for almost eight years fighting Mussolini's futile war. This, along with the ravages of war, left a gaping, raw hole in her life from the ages of twelve to twenty. It was something that she never forgot.

Daniel ended up in Italy after the war. He met Giulia at a dance in Rome, and they soon fell in love. After three years of courtship, Daniel left for the promise of America to pursue the legendary dream. He settled in a small room in the Upper West Side. Giulia quickly followed, and they both worked brutal hours in the Garment District with a combined income of $72 per week.

After saving what they could over the years, they moved into an apartment in Forest Hills, Queens. Daniels's big break came when a friend from Yugoslavia made it out of Europe with all his money and commissioned Daniel to build him a house on Long Island. Being an architect, Daniel did an inspired job and, with the money earned from his design work, bought a house in Forest Hills for $18,000. Giulia sold it after Daniel's death for a huge profit.

Daniel got another job through another war friend at the Swiss electrical engineering company, Brown Boveri, where his command of six languages made him an asset, and his work ethic and character made him invaluable. Meanwhile, given her fluency in Italian, Giulia got a job at the U.S. headquarters of Fiat.

The couple was prudent and careful, and they did quite well for themselves financially by making wise investments in stocks, such as banking early in the gene whizzes of Genentech—often cited as one of the best stock picks ever—and buying and flipping real estate. From nothing to something of substance—literally the embodiment of the American Dream.

***

Margaret's bold move asking me to marry her had me thrilled but also forced me to ask myself questions. Given my history making life moves that sometimes left me wondering why I did what I did, I had to drill down and ask the toughest one: *Was I in love with her, or was I just in lust with her?* While we had known each other for some time and I'd sacrificed my previous relationship for her, we'd really only been intimate for three weeks. Knowing someone at work and lusting after them is one thing but dating and the closeness it brings put us on a whole new level of intensity.

While my decision to leave Molly was made with some reflection, I felt there hadn't been that much to lose with a bad move. Losing Molly wasn't a huge loss. Losing Margaret though, despite not knowing her anywhere near as long, would have been devastating to me. Marrying her was a huge risk for me, given my past. Lucy had been a mistake, no question about it. But now the chance presented itself again, and I had a choice to make. I'd made some bad decisions in my life, but when I chose to take Margaret's offer to get married, I had a deep-seated confidence that it was the right thing to do—perhaps the most right thing I'd ever done. Turns out history has proven me correct. After all these years I can safely say marrying Margaret was the best decision of my life.

***

We moved into her doorman building on Yellowstone and Queens Boulevard in Forest Hills. I never had a doorman and felt very successful having someone open my door for me morning and evening and say, "Hello Mr. Roberts." I felt like a real swell.

We remained the top two sales people at Kraft, and Stan Saperstein paid us well. I had never made that kind of money before—sixty thousand including bonuses—which was damn good money in 1989, even in New York City. I was thirty-three, with great money, a successful career, respect in my field and status as a well-regarded chess Master. I had a beautiful, cultured, brilliant wife, a snazzy apartment, and I lived in the most exciting city in the world. I'd done all of that with a ninth-grade education.

Unfortunately, while this would be heaven on earth for most, my undiagnosed bipolar disorder wouldn't allow happiness for more than a fleeting moment. I also had other outward issues that I couldn't hide with a fake smile.

I had a bad temper.

This was not just irritability or snippiness or an occasional ill-timed outburst. Rather, I would get in big fights with my co-workers—not fistfights, but the occasional unhinged, vein-popping screaming match. Had I not been the number one salesperson by a long ways, I probably would have been fired. My behavior sometimes was appalling, and it was only my outsized worth to the company that people put up with my shit. Bobby Knight and Woody Hayes could also be stark-raving ass-holes at times, but nobody wanted to fire them because they delivered the goods. Me too.

Oh, wait, they did get fired. But I didn't.

I also got into fights while playing chess in Washington Square Park. Sure, chess can be a stressful competition, but I would sometimes completely lose my shit and make a scene right out of a movie. I would go into depressions, and then I'd come out of them in the grip of a mania that would come over me like wildfire, overtaking a deer in the forest, and the madness would consume every thought. During these times, I'd go off into manic Crazy Town and would concoct all kinds of crackpot, unrealistic ideas.

While some were money-making ideas or notions about people or conspiracies or what was wrong with the world and how I could fix it, mostly it would just entail fantasies of running away. I would create detailed itineraries of where I'd go and exactly how I'd do it and the steps I'd take to do it. These times left me emotionally unavailable to my co-workers and, worse, to Margaret. For some reason, my perfect destination had me running away to Los Angeles. Why Los Angeles? I don't know. It wasn't like I was a Lakers or Dodgers fan. Hardly. Plus, it seemed awfully sunny, and I had the idea that everyone referred to each other as "Dude," like right out of a surfer film. Maybe Los Angeles just seemed the farthest place I could go. If I'd actually followed through on Los Angeles, I'm sure I soon would have had an obsession on running away to Alaska. Then China, and so on.

Next...Mars?

My mother always handled any problem she had with Ralph by running away, and so, as a child, running away was ingrained into my coping skills as the go-to solution. It sure made sense for my mother although it played hell on her kids and, truth be told, on her, too. Margaret knew something was wrong with me, but in 1989 mental illness was not quite so easily recognizable as it is today. People were aware of it, certainly, but it was still a subject you shied away from and hoped would just "get better." It didn't.

CHAPTER TWELVE

An Opening for Attack

*"The single most important thing in life is to believe
in yourself regardless of what everyone else says."*
—Hikaru Nakamura, U.S. Chess Grandmaster

Fate has a funny way of making decisions for you. I received a call
from a friend back in Baltimore, and it shook me to my core.

"Did you know Albert Gunther had been sold?" he asked me.

Those words stunned me. What he said couldn't be possible, could
it? Gunther had been *the* hardware store in midtown Baltimore for
almost seventy years. It was an institution in that town and was such a
landmark people joked they'd built Baltimore around Gunther. It took
me a moment to answer.

"They *sold* Gunther's? You're not joking? They *sold* it?"

"Yeah," he continued, "the new management's moving Gunther out
into the suburbs."

I instantly knew this was a big mistake. Home Depot and Hechinger
were in the suburbs. Home Depot was a rising giant in the home
improvement business, and Hechinger was the old, experienced player
on the scene. But just because Hechinger had been around a long time
didn't make them quaint. On the contrary, the Maryland-based home
improvement titan had been founded in 1911 and, by that time, had
many dozens of large, modern big-box stores all around the area. My

feelings about Gunther's move to the 'burbs to compete with the big boys like Home Depot, Hechinger and Lowe's was that they were making a catastrophic misreading of their market. They were also abdicating a big chunk of business they should be owning. All the major design firms and architectural firms were in downtown Baltimore, and I knew that, by moving away from that prime area, they'd be leaving a lot of money on the table.

I got off the phone, my gears spinning. There would be a huge void now for decorative door hardware in Baltimore, specifically downtown. Sure, the high-end downtown customers could travel to the suburbs to do business, but why should they have to do that? As the minutes ticked by, an idea formed. Being bipolar can have its terrible drawbacks, but there are moments when it is a godsend. It allows you to conceptualize without fear of failure or cautious regard for pitfalls. During these times, it's as if your desktop computer—for short bursts—could become a mainframe computer, working at many times normal speed. I can't explain how or why that happens but there are moments it gives you flashes of "*I can take over the world*" confidence, but it's not just a warm sense of megalomania but thoughts that are expressed on logical, connective dots that, for those however brief flashes, give you the path to making whatever it is actually happen. For those short stretches, your mind allows you to think ten moves deep. I knew what I had to do now. I would open a decorative hardware and plumbing store in Baltimore.

I finally had enough of the plan in my head to bring it to the High Council: Margaret. If she didn't like it, this would pose a problem. How could such an audacious plan happen without her blessing? Answer: it couldn't.

I mentally prepped and took her aside. She was about to experience one of the three best sales pitches I ever did in my life. My two best pitches would come later.

Fortunately, she loved it. I'm blessed Margaret is not a wild risk-taker, like me (she's a pragmatist, thank God!), but she's no wimp, and so if she thought it was a good idea...it was a *good idea*. She has a spine of steel (she clearly comes from strong stock), so she embraced it immediately, and we began laying plans.

We decided to sell our apartment and take our life savings to gamble on opening our new business. We had come up with a name and used it in my pitch: Designer's Hardware. We liked the ring of it, and it sounded appropriately professional. She recognized the opportunity despite the potential risks but believed in us and warmed to the idea, as I laid out how we'd do it.

Once the idea was out there, it sort of took on a life of its own and, despite the fate of Albert Gunther & Co., we actually began spit balling different locations other than Baltimore where it might work. We considered Atlanta and a few other locations, but we kept coming back to Baltimore. That was the place, for many reasons, we figured we could be the most successful.

At Kraft, Margaret and I were the two top salespeople and figured between us we could handle anything related to hardware. I had learned the decorative plumbing business from Stan Saperstein, and I strongly believed the concepts Stan had implemented and perfected in New York City could work back in Baltimore. To get the plan rolling, I knew we needed a commitment from the leading designer in Baltimore to give us his business if we were going to make the move back to Baltimore and open up our own store.

My target was Alexander Baer, the owner of Alexander Baer Associates in Baltimore. If he would commit to giving us his business, the other designers would likely give us their business as well. Not that I thought she needed it, but with such an important commitment, I knew this would give Margaret an even higher comfort level in taking the plunge of going into business ourselves. Alex Baer was a short, kind man, with a gentle demeanor who treated everyone graciously. He was one of the classiest people I have ever known.

Alex had worked with me years earlier during my days at Gunther's, and we had a great relationship. He'd even call me from Baltimore to purchase items from Kraft when he couldn't find a product in Baltimore.

Alexander Baer had the crème de la crème of Baltimore high society and that mostly meant the rich Jews, particularly in Pikesville, a predominantly Jewish section of Baltimore. Over the years, anecdotes leaked out about how rich his customers were, but I never completely confirmed them. It was rumored that Alexander charged *one hundred thousand dollars* per room to decorate your home. I could never confirm this number or any other rumors because the price and specific details about Alex's business were like a state secret—no one ever wanted to admit they'd paid that much, but the legendary price alone gave the buyer great cachet. Working with Alex Baer exemplified the famous old saw *If you have to ask the price...*

With Baltimore having one of the largest Jewish communities in the country, if you wanted to do well selling luxury products in that city, you needed to have Jewish clients. The Jewish clique was very tight knit, and if you did well with a handful of clients, word would spread like wildfire, and, soon, you'd have them all. Aside from offering the best fixtures and equipment, you would also need to give them fair pricing and outstanding, white-glove service, but in return they would reward you with fervent loyalty through a booming return business and plenty of referrals. It was the perfect storm for me to go into business, and I saw it as plain as day.

I went to the linchpin of my plan and told Alex Baer exactly what I had in mind and that it could take me a year to fully set up business in Baltimore.

"But, if I have your commitment to giving me your business, I'm willing to take the risk."

Alex smiled. "Troy, take your time. One year, two years, three years, doesn't matter. When you and Margaret get down here, you'll have my business. And you can literally take that to the bank."

That's all I needed. I began taking Margaret on trips to Baltimore, to familiarize her with my city and visit Uncle Jake and Aunt Peggy. I wanted her to feel a part of the city and having family as an anchor, regardless of their past, would be a good inducement, especially since I had a great relationship with Uncle Jake and Aunt Peggy. It worked, as Margaret grew to love Baltimore. Designer's Hardware, Inc. was not just a good idea any more. It was now a real thing.

CHAPTER THIRTEEN

After the Opening Moves

"You may learn much more from a game you lose than from a game you win."
—José Raúl Capablanca,

Cuban World Champion Grandmaster

Now that we had given birth to the idea of Designer's Hardware and it was a fragile newborn, we now needed to raise it properly. It took us a few months to get our feet under us, but in 1989 Margaret and I took the leap and bought a two-story building on Read Street in an artsy neighborhood of Baltimore. We were three blocks from Alexander Baer's office and within walking distance of at least a dozen design and architecture firms. Ironically, we were also pretty much across the street from my old alma mater, Albert Gunther, but they were transitioning out of the neighborhood.

We were poised for success. We opened a very cozy (read: tiny) showroom on the first floor and lived on the second floor. This was a business model historically used by so many from the dawn of America's Industrial Age onwards: to own a business and have a place to live while surviving in the big city. From laundries and butcher shops to delis and restaurants, so many built their fortunes by living in their first investment in America. Real estate costs in Baltimore, compared to NYC, were comparatively cheap so we decided it was best to own our own building. But after buying the building and paying for displays, inventory and distributorships of the best product lines in the plumbing and hardware industry, we had a mere six thousand bucks left to our name. Once we'd counted our pennies and realized we were mere nickels and dimes and one crisis away from being destitute, new-business owners, there was some strain that might have caused some sleepless nights.

Fortunately, we had a Fairy Godfather, so our anxiety over that skinny safety margin only lasted about ten minutes. True to his word, Alexander Bear immediately showered us with an embarrassment of riches and, in the wave of his wand, gave us almost more business than we could handle. Another stroke of luck happened when Margaret contacted a friend, a designer in New York City who just happened to be working with a client who had made the massively lucrative Time-Warner merger happen. The client was building a twenty-five-million-dollar home on Long Island. Margaret's designer friend ended up purchasing over one-hundred-and-fifty-thousand dollars in faucets and door hardware from us.

Manna from heaven.

I had a great idea to market the shop. A newspaper article!

I made a least twenty-five calls to the Baltimore Sun requesting an article and finally succeeded.

On July 2, 1989, the *Baltimore Sun* did a charming article in the Maryland Living section on us and our little shop. The article was on the front page of the popular Sunday section and was filled with details and featured a photo of the two of us in our store. The article really helped solidify the image of Designer's Hardware, Inc. as the go-to place for interesting and hot fixtures. Despite being small, Designer's Hardware was on top of the latest trends and could find items for you that few, if any others, could do.

We began getting regular retail customers who wanted upscale hardware and plumbing products not available in the big-box stores. Back then, Home Depot and Lowe's only offered standard contractor-grade stuff, primarily cheap hardware and cheap faucets. Not exactly schlock, but it wasn't anything like what we carried. Their stuff was mostly the kinds of items you'd put into dime-a-dozen tract houses in the suburbs or rentals. We wanted to establish Designer's Hardware, Inc. as the place to buy the "good stuff." Uncle Jake was very proud I'd become a business owner and not a lunch bag man despite my having to conform to regular hours. In his eyes, no lunch bag man could be the boss of his own domain, so I got a pass. He would stop by and plop down at Margaret's desk, waiting to tell anyone who walked in, in his best Baltimorese, "You gotta look at dem New York styles dey got here!"

Despite Uncle Jake seeming a little discordant among the sophistication and shi-shi fixtures we offered, he added a particular charming brand of color that amused people. Around that time, we also had a revelation that was even bigger than the move to start Designer's Hardware. Margaret was pregnant. We were thrilled. Between the excitement of the new business and the impending new member of our family, it was a wonderful time for us.

It seemed during that period every time we turned around there was some new-found bounty in our lives. At a birthing class in Maryland General Hospital, Margaret and I met a young couple. The husband owned a small glass-and-mirror business he had just started. Knowing what the newspaper article had done for our fledgling business, I insisted he call the reporter from the *Baltimore Sun* who had written our piece. I told him to tell the reporter he knew me and that he should write an article on their new business.

Unlike me, who doesn't know what the words "give up" mean, he gave up trying after a few calls when the reporter didn't return his calls.

I was adamant. "Keep calling everyday," I insisted. "You'll get him."

I added, "Call like your business and future depend on it."

While it might have sounded hyperbolic to a casual observer, I truly believed that. To his credit, he listened, and after several weeks of hounding the reporter, the guy finally responded and did a huge spread on his glass-and-mirror business in the same Maryland Living section our piece appeared.

He received so much business after the article he could barely handle it.

He later told me the article was easily worth several hundred thousand dollars in new business. With this huge jump start catapulting him to early success, he would later grow to become a major player in Baltimore's glass-and-mirror scene. We cultivated our relationship and sent customers each other's way.

As for Designer's Hardware, we did over $500,000 our first year in business and $800,000 our second year, astounding numbers given they were generated out of less than 700 square feet of showroom. Despite the demands of the business, I still found time for chess tournaments and, having honed my game over such stiff competition in New York, I had improved considerably. My chess rating skyrocketed to 2339, and I feared no player in Baltimore or Washington.

In one tournament in D.C., I took on one of my toughest opponents, and it sounds crazy, but he was just a child. But what a child! He was the youngest rated chess Master in the country since Bobby Fischer and, while his trainer and parents looked on, I spanked him and sent him packing. Defeating Josh Waitzkin, the prodigy the book and movie *Searching for Bobby Fischer* was based upon, was quite a highlight for my chess career. Yeah, he was twelve or thirteen at the time, but he was also a very dangerous player and easily crushed most adults, so I was proud of my victory.

***

Clara Annabell Roberts was born on Valentine's Day, February 14, 1990. It should have been a wildly happy time for us, but Margaret's father, Daniel, was dying of cancer and that dimmed our joyous moment. Margaret's folks had bought an apartment a few blocks from the showroom to be near Margaret. Daniel saw that Baltimore property was really cheap compared to New York real estate, so he bought another apartment in the same building as an investment despite my attempts to dissuade him. I tried to talk him out of it, reminding him this was Baltimore, not Manhattan, and the chances of him making money by buying and selling property, like he did in New York, were small.

I could see the cancer was stressing his ability to think clearly and despite my warnings, he went ahead and bought the place. He did get to see his granddaughter but, sadly, left us within two months after Clara was born. I remember thinking that, with the amazing life he led, all of the sights he'd seen and experiences he'd had, all the cities of the world he had been to and lived in, it seemed like such an anticlimax that he died in Baltimore, Maryland, on Saint Paul Street.

Margaret's mom soldiered on and helped us by caring for baby Clara during the day while Margaret and I worked the showroom at Designer's Hardware. One of the last things Daniel had done before dying was to rent out the investment apartment in his building to a young black man. All his references had checked out, but he turned out to be a scam artist. Because of Baltimore's rental laws, once a renter gets into an apartment it can be a lengthy and difficult process to evict them. The guy turned out to be a master at working that system. At first, Margaret and her mother were secretive about this deadbeat, keeping the details from me out of fear over what I might do. He had already bounced three checks and had no intention of ever making good on them. He'd found a free ride and wasn't going to get off the merry-go-round. He was going to stay in that apartment, for free, as long as he could. They hid from me what was going on, but it was really only a matter of time until I found out. Frankly, due to the unstable nature of my bipolar, their fears were well-founded.

Finally, it got too far out of control, and Margaret screwed up her courage and spilled the beans about the rental scam the guy was pulling on her mother. Bipolar can be a dangerous condition, and, on many occasions in my life, I had lost my temper completely. This was one of those occasions. Margaret had suggested that we start eviction proceedings but, in my mind, I would rather confront and threaten him like a raving maniac. After absorbing the story and realizing I was dealing with someone who had no intentions of relenting or making good on his debt, I knew what I was going to do, and nothing would stop me. He needed to be dealt with without quarter, something I would do to any chess opponent who was so reckless as to leave himself so vulnerable.

I drove to my mother-in-law's apartment building and rapped on the door of the con man. The door cracked enough for us to size each other up. He was tall, thick and very dark. He stared balefully at me through the slit. Then, he unhooked the chain, stood to full height, as if to intimidate me as I gave up several inches to him.

He growled in a challenging tone, "Yeah? What do you want?"

"You need to make arrangements to move out of my mother-in-law's apartment tomorrow," I said matter-of-factly. My tone was cold but even. The man looked at me as if I were nuts and let out a loud guffaw.

"You gotta be fuckin' kiddin'!" He started to close the door, and my foot stopped it. My face was stony, but my voice was still polite but icily firm.

"No. I'm not. You need to make the arrangements to move out tomorrow."

The guy looked at me as if I were stupid and shook his head in disbelief. "Fuck you! Hell no! I'm not going anywhere. Now get the fuck outta here!"

That's all I needed. I whipped the .38 handgun from my belt and shoved it hard against his cheek.

"Wrong answer."

I shoved the door wide and jammed my gun deep into his ribs.

He looked more surprised than afraid. I think, at that point, he was street smart enough to see a bluff. Or at least that's what he assumed. He would have been wrong. Dead wrong.

He was aware enough to see that the man with the gun was serious. Or crazy. Or both. He read my eyes and had enough smarts to realize his perception of a bluff just might be a fatal one. He stepped back away from me and began to talk me down. He said, "Hey man, your name's Troy, right?"

"Yes. Troy." My answer was flat, robotic.

"Shit, Troy, don't be stupid, you have too much to lose."

"How do you know my name? I don't know you."

"I know all about you" he said, his manner now almost obsequious, a condition clearly triggered by mortal fear. He began talking fast, but you could tell he was choosing his words very carefully. As if his life depended on it.

"You just had a baby, opened a small business, and you're a chess Master. Right? I mean, man, you gotta be smart to be one of those, a chess guy, right?"

The man's eyes widened, and I'm sure the cynical side of his brain was shoved aside by his fearful, pragmatic brain, as it rushed to create a fast-forward, time-lapse movie in his mind.

"Troy, man, listen, this is a big mistake."

"You had your chance. This is the last time you'll ever fuck someone out of their hard-earned savings."

At this point, he erupted in both flop-sweat and a sea of words meant to ingratiate himself with me. He used my name over and over, just as Sigourney Weaver had taught me, and I couldn't help but think that this jackoff could be a good salesman...if he wasn't such a failure as a criminal. He began to hyperventilate in terror as he carefully and with great authenticity explained how he'd seen the error of his ways and would never, ever do such a thing again.

Despite his breathless entreaties, I calmly explained in a voice that sounded as warm as broken glass, "You are fucking with the wrong white boy."

"I know, I know!" he bleated, but he didn't know. He had no fuck-ing idea how I'd grown up, how people with bipolar can't always control their better angels and how utterly dangerous I could be, if provoked. I was Granddaddy Noonan's grandson and had Granddaddy Noonan's batshit madman's blood flowing through me. I also had inherited Granddaddy Noonan's powerful mind-fucking affliction, which was the big fat cherry on the psychologist's sundae. That meant I was capable of anything, like run a hardware store by day and "handle a problem" by night. It meant I could be completely crazy and yet not know the reason why. I was in the grip of the madness that came over me, but he kept Sigourney Weavering me with my name, and that eventually threw me off.

"Troy," he whined, "please, for God's sake, put your gun away. You and I will forget this ever happened. Never happened my friend. Troy, I'll move out this week. I swear to God. I'm gone."

I considered his plea for a moment. Perhaps some of my Angel of Death character had faded a bit, as I was suddenly open to reason.

"If I did let you live, you'd just go to the police. Right?"

"There's no fucking way I'll rat you out to the cops, Troy. I'm telling you."

"'Cause if you report me to the police, you realize I'll get out on bail and come back and finish the job? I'll kill you deader than dogshit, and there won't be a thing you can do to stop me. I'll put a bullet in your brain and chop you up in little bite-sized pieces and throw you in a big, black garbage bag and put what's left down real fuckin' deep. Knowing that, will you move out of my mother-in-law's apartment immediately? And keep your fucking mouth shut?"

"Absolutely, Troy. Let's forget this ever happened, and I swear I won't say a thing. Not a thing! I mean it Troy. This never happened!"

After a few moments of thought, I looked him straight in the eyes with a pretty convincing 'don't fuck with me' gaze Granddaddy Noonan would have approved of, put the gun into my waistband and walked away.

He kept his word about not going to the police, but not about leaving the apartment. After I realized that he had no intention of moving any time soon, my murderous inclinations gave way to reason, and we set the eviction process in motion the conventional way with the Maryland District Court. After approximately six weeks, he was formally evicted. The day finally came when his furniture and belongings were put out on the sidewalk for the neighborhood scavengers...and, as a message to him, he came home to his shit on the sidewalk, a locked door and less possessions than a homeless man living under a bridge.

In the You-Gotta-Be-Outta-Your-Mind Dept., he actually had the brass to come to Designer's Hardware after being ejected to register his objection and forcefully express his displeasure over being unceremoniously thrown onto the pavement. I just laughed and told him, "Get out of my store."

***

Two years passed, and all was well. The store was a success, and Margaret and I were enjoying the early stages of parenthood and the daily joys with a little one. But, typical of my disorder, there was always the bipolar axiom, the little voice in the back of the mind saying, *"You've got a good thing...change it!"* Perhaps I chafed at the fact that everything was going so nicely. Yet I also felt limited, as if some part of my vision for Designer's Hardware was unrealized, that we were somehow missing out on something. I got it into my head that I needed to raise capital by selling half of the business and use the money to expand into a much larger showroom. Margaret didn't see the need to upend the system we had, because it was working well. She also acknowledged that, once I got the bug, it was hard—if not impossible—to stop me.

One of my clients was Arthur, a wealthy young man from Texas . Arthur was a short man, no more than five foot- three inches tall, and barely more than one hundred ten pounds, but his wallet was much bigger. He'd renovated a sprawling, historic townhouse in Bolton Hill and purchased all his plumbing and door hardware from me. We became friends over time, and I knew he had an interest in my world of hardware. Needing cash for my planned expansion, I just came right out one day and asked if he would like to be our partner. In my extended sales pitch, I played on his fascination for the decorative hardware business and took him to the premier showrooms in Washington, D.C., including Union Hardware in Bethesda and the Kraft Showroom in the Washington Design Center. (Stan Saperstein had since opened that Kraft branch in D.C.) I explained that Baltimore deserved a high-end showroom, and there was a lot of money to be made.

Some people who inherit money, because they had it handed to them, don't really know its value. The so-called idiot sons (and daughters). Arthur was not one of them. He was definitely interested, but he was also a tough negotiator and knew the value—and power—of his wealth. He later told me the key to great negotiating is your ability to say no to any deal and walk away. Millions in the bank made that a whole lot easier. He was the perfect example of never playing poker with scared money. With his dough, he didn't need to do a damn thing. He'd be just fine if nothing changed, thank you very much. Arthur was certainly willing to walk away from the table and take his chips elsewhere. I accepted every demand he made. If I had been willing to walk away from the deal, I might have made more money, but I was inpatient and got what I needed: money. This new deal gave me the capital not only to expand our showroom but to buy a five-bedroom house in Roland Park.

I was extremely impulsive and, while it often created worry and hardship for Margaret, it turned out I was often right. I was able to rationalize many of my seemingly reckless moves by citing how many times successful people were mocked and derided for their revolutionary ideas, that is until those ideas proved correct and they shot to the moon.

But sometimes my impulsiveness—when applied on a less megalomaniacal scale—made for a happy ending without any journey of stress and strain. I met a designer named Felicia, in her early fifties with a lovely, oval face and deep, brown eyes that looked almost black and elegant silver hair. She looked like a model for products for women of that age, because she had an ageless beauty most women never possess, let alone at more than half a century. We became friends, and I discovered she had no partner in life despite yearning for one. This left me perplexed, because she was so beautiful. Of course, given my fixation on making any and all things run efficiently around me, I saw this as yet another conundrum that needed addressing. When Felicia actually came right out and asked me if I knew of anyone, I could introduce to her, I knew I had to do something about it, but then, after taking her number with a promise to act on her behalf, I got caught up in the intricacies of life and business and let it slide.

Several months later, the father-in-law of a friend of Margaret's was visiting Baltimore from New York. He was a classy guy in his late seventies and a very successful entrepreneur who had banked millions. He took Margaret, Margaret's friend, his son and me to a lavish dinner at The Prime Rib.

He and I chatted, and he was fascinated I owned my own business. We talked about entrepreneurship and the vagaries and triumphs of business but soon the discussion became personal, and he mentioned how lonely he was. This was where my bipolar impulses could be focused for a simple good deed. With a flash of an idea, I excused myself and ran to the phone booth to make a phone call.

I called Felicia and told her about this millionaire who was eating with me at The Prime Rib. I told her he was a great guy, funny, smart... and lonely. She demurred on jumping in her car and racing down to meet him, but rather invited us to visit her at her home. I returned to the table and told him my game plan. He was up for it, so after dinner we all drove up to Lutherville, Maryland, on the north side of Baltimore to visit Felicia.

The rest of us chatted quietly as the two would-be lovebirds began talking. They talked for hours. As the evening passed, the rest of us were amused and delighted they seemed to have clicked so well. Two people totally engrossed in each other and so apparently well-matched. They fell in love and, for a while, maintained a long-distance courtship. They held their marriage at the Belvedere Hotel. It was magnificent! In the middle of the festivities, Felicia's new husband got up and proclaimed me, "The Messenger from God," for bringing them together. Nah, I'm just an impulse-driven, bipolar matchmaker.

***

To expand our business, our new partner, Arthur, and I bought the old Hair Garage building on Read Street, across from the tiny show-room where Designer's Hardware started. We set about with a grand vision and soon created a stunning showroom that rivaled any in New York or Washington. Over the next four years, we averaged at least $2 million dollars a year in decorative hardware and plumbing supplies. Sure, it was a bigger operation than the old Designer's Hardware, but it grossed a whole lot more. My idea to grow the business had been validated.

Again, I had proven to all who could see that I had it all. A smart, beautiful wife, a cute and precocious daughter, a thriving business with a partner I trusted and a house in one of the most prestigious neigh-borhoods in Baltimore. I was living alongside the doctors, lawyers and CEOs that had gone to Baltimore's finest schools and the world's best universities. With a mere ninth-grade education, I felt pride that I had accomplished my version of the American Dream. I had become a suc-cess and left the notion of ever being a lunch bag man far, far in my tail lights.

And, yet, I was not happy.

I had this indefinable restlessness. It was a tiny stone in my shoe, a small but sharp stabbing that nagged at me day and night and gave me no peace or the ability to enjoy what I so obviously had in front of me. It was like being at a buffet of the finest food and someone had put some-thing sour in each dish to ruin the flavor. Despite my embarrassment of riches, I just wanted to sell my half of the business and run away. My untreated bipolar condition made me unstable.

So unstable I decided I'd do it right this time. I'd do suicide right.

***

The turmoil in my mind was there and there alone. My life was good, even great, and yet I felt the overpowering drive to end it, to escape the torment. The voices in my head were clear: it's your only way out. Out of what the voices didn't specify, but they didn't need to clarify. I was on board. The voices were right. I had to go.

They say the third time's the charm, and that was one of my blackly comedic thoughts, as I put a single bullet in my pocket and climbed down the stairs to our basement. Mostly, though, I was acting mechanically, like I was about to perform a simple task that required no thought, like taking out the trash. My decision had been made, and all that was left was to execute the final step. I figured the basement would be easier for Margaret to clean up afterward. The massive permutations of the misery I would cause and long-term effects on my loved ones and those who knew me were not really in my thoughts. Had they been, I likely never would have made one step toward those stairs. But here I was, and I was ready.

With a typical, stark, solitary naked light bulb illuminating the basement, I sat on the cement floor and lifted the gun and looked it over a moment. My ticket out of the madness. I opened the cylinder, took the cartridge from my pocket, inserted it and spun the cylinder to at least give me some odds. Had I wanted to just end it quickly with no drama, I would have a used an automatic, not a revolver. Even to the end, I wanted the theatrics of Russian roulette and a final bet. As a guy who'd spent more than a few dollars and hours calculating odds, both in gambling and chess, I thought about my one-in-six chance and snapped the cylinder shut.

I was ready. I put the gun to my temple and cocked the hammer. It was ready to rock and blow my brains out. Lights out, sayonara, hasta la vista.

I pulled the trigger.

CLICK.

It was the loudest insignificant metal-on-metal sound I'd ever heard. Not dead yet, as Monty Python would say.

One in six. Had I beaten the odds? Was that a sign? Did I really want to die?

A cold sweat suddenly engulfed me, as if a chilly humidifier had come on right next to me, and icy sweat ran down me. In seconds. It's the only time that's ever happened. I've played sports for hours and not sweated as much as I did in those scant seconds. Was this a message from some part of my brain, my conscience, my id, somewhere deep inside with which I wasn't directly in touch? Was I supposed to be dead now, or was I supposed to get the hell off the floor and take care of business and my family and live a life?

I stood, shook it off and went upstairs to Margaret and Clara.

I would never again try to take my life.

***

We had twelve employees, and they had no idea which Troy would show up for work on any given day. The sweet, charming guy who used your name a lot and cared about you as a person or the rage-a-holic, psycho asshole who'd fly off the handle at the slightest provocation in defiance of all logic. That roll-the-dice quality made working for me a stressful and miserable proposition. Poor Arthur had no idea what he had gotten into going into business with me.

The classic, crazy person in movies thinks they're Napoleon or Catherine the Great. Not me. One day, I wanted to write a book or screenplay based on my life. The next, I was buying a vending-machine-and-gumball route to add another business to my portfolio. God only knows how and why, in a manic state, I bought a gumball-and-vending-machine route across the city. It was the classic example of stumbling over the dollars to pick up the pennies. I would leave work after a long day at Designer's Hardware and spend hours driving around loading the vending machines at night. It was batshit personified. I would run myself into the ground working the vending machine route for maybe an extra grand a month. This made no practical sense, because I could dip into the cash register at Designer's Hardware and pocket a thousand a month without it even being missed.

After a while chasing my tail with that time-sapping route, I thanked God when I found a builder friend interested in buying it from me. I just couldn't remain focused, and it played hell with those closest to me. My ping-ponging from one thing to another vexed poor Margaret to no end. She was never sure from one day to the next what nutty idea I'd chase. I'd be motoring along with my usual ups-and-downs. Then, I'd have a major manic episode. This meant change had to occur or else.

Granted, when a bipolar person gets manic, they can be enormously creative and author some truly great ideas. Still, they often desperately need a mediating force to push back with a position of reason, a person who is a more rational, down-to-earth influence to channel their mania, however brilliant, and not let them go too far.

Fly to the sun?

Hmmm. How 'bout we just go to the moon? Probably a better chance of success, and we won't be burned to a crisp.

From my point of view, I could do no wrong and was thus inspired to reach for the stars. The gravity of reality be damned. I can DO IT! In those times when the mania enveloped me, I was a golden boy, a super-star incapable of error. There was nothing that I could not accomplish. I had a vision to change an entire industry!

And I did.

But it cost me almost everything.

CHAPTER FOURTEEN

Genius Moves

"Genius. It's a word. What does it really mean? If I win I'm a genius. If I don't, I'm not."
—Bobby Fischer

Being bipolar can often be likened to driving through life without the limiting effects of brakes. You plot a direction and go full bore toward it, but you have no way to slow down, let alone stop. It's the antithesis of chess strategy to play with complete abandon. In chess, it makes no sense and leads to a rapid loss of pieces and a quick mate, but in life it sometimes—especially if you're bipolar—can seem plausible, even reasonable. With all that I had, I would do absolutely crazy things, nothing a sane man with a family and the responsibilities of a business would do.

One of my employees, Harold, a genteel black man, came to me and explained that his car was being held for ransom at an auto body shop although he'd paid his repair bill in full. The body shop was on East North Avenue in a tough, black section of the city. I told Harold not to worry. We would get his car back.

To look as intimidating as possible, I put on my black leather aviator jacket. I also brought along a little additional intimidation: my .38. We drove over to the body shop and strode into the office with my gun tucked into my belt. The owner looked up from the desk and recognized Harold.

"You bring me more money, you sorry-ass motherfucker?"

Harold shook his head. "No. I brought something better. Him."

The body shop owner gave me his best baleful gaze. "What's your excuse, motherfucker?"

I opened my jacket and displayed the stock of gun.

"I don't need an excuse. I got this. Now give us his fucking keys."

I could see this level of conflict was unexpected and startled the man. He stood slowly and took some keys off a pegboard behind him and held them out. He didn't look too happy, but his initial bluster had vanished. Harold took his keys. As we walked out to our cars, I heard the owner bitching to one of his employees, "You b'lieve that motherfucker brought five-oh to clean up his shit?"

***

The mind of someone who is bipolar is a thing to behold. It can be as calm and peaceful as a mill pond in summer, its surface like glass. It can also fly into bizarre flights that would make a geologist's seismometer during a tectonic shift look like a flat line. Those are the times the ideas or thoughts that explode from the psyche of the afflicted can seem nothing short of mad, the deranged harum-scarum ideations of someone who is untethered to everyone else's reality. Yet, the thoughts seems quite logical to the person with mania, even incontrovertibly essential. There are other times the crazy ideas just happened to be truly inspired, once slower minds have a chance to catch up and evaluate what has been put forth.

My idea was brilliantly simple, one of those great ideas that leave you wondering why no one else saw it. Like finding a trail of gold coins on the ground and simply following them and putting them in your pocket. My showroom and similar showrooms across the county sold high-end products to people in the top two percent of income. What if the top echelon of the country's earners and consumers of high-end hardware were exposed to those high-end decorative products in stores, other than just limited, specialty environments?

In other words, what if they were more accessible? Like *a lot* more accessible? Since accessibility breeds greater sales and greater sales breeds competition and lower prices, why wouldn't such a concept be possibly the next best thing to sliced bread? I was sure lots more people and not just the really well-to-do would buy the home jewelry we sold, if they happened to be in their local big box versus that fancy schmancy (read: pricey) specialty shop across town. At that time, burgeoning big box stores, like Home Depot, Lowe's and Hechinger, sold only cheap and sometimes mid-grade hardware and plumbing fixtures. This was chintzy contractor-grade stuff of a quality that designers wouldn't touch with fire tongs.

My plan was to strike a deal with one of the big box stores to open Designer's Hardware concessions in their stores. It was audacious, but I knew it would succeed, and I would make a killing. I approached Arthur with my idea, but he was not as enthusiastic as I had hoped he would be. Arthur was conservative in his approach to business (as big money often is) and felt we should remain focused on our business model and keep building market share. His reasoning was that my plan, while having a sizable potential upside (*potential* being the operative term), would distract us from the business we'd started and were growing steadily. He was trying to convey the dog-and-the-bone scenario to me, but I wouldn't have such small thinking.

The only thing that gave Arthur and Margaret some solace was that they weren't too concerned with my latest tangent ever going anywhere. They really didn't see any realistic way for me to make any of it happen. They figured it was more pie-in-the-sky from Troy, so they indulged me by ignoring me. What they didn't count on was that, during a manic period, a bipolar person can make things happen no one expects. Go to the top of Everest? Build the atomic bomb? Discover fire? Yes, they scoffed. But my idea was not good, it was great, and I was going to walk right past their patronage and show them. Never assume that a bipolar person cannot execute their seemingly preposterous out-of-reach idea. They might just surprise you.

***

First, ignoring the naysayers, I began planning who to approach. Home Depot was obvious because they were the biggest, but they were too far away, headquartered in Atlanta. I felt I needed a corporate HQ that was closer, so I could closely watch and nurture any seeds that were planted. Lowe's was based in North Carolina, so again I was concerned about the distance. Then I came to Hechinger. The third-largest home center big box with 145 stores, their head office was in Landover, Maryland, just a stone's throw away.

I put Hechinger in my sights. Next, I had to come up with a pitch that got people foaming at the mouth over my concept. Then, I needed an introduction to get in the room with their brass to knock their socks off with this yet-to-be-created dazzling pitch. Carolyn, a well-heeled client with whom I'd become good friends, believed in me, and when I told her my brainstorm, she immediately jumped on board. Her plan was to dig around, find out who owned a lot of Hechinger stock, convince them to hear my pitch and vouch for us with Hechinger. Once she found a large stockholder, she was sure she could get me an introduction to the company.

When Carolyn took up my cause with great zeal, I knew she was smart enough and savvy enough to make it happen. Carolyn did some poking around and found out that the venerable old Baltimore brokerage house, Alex. Brown & Sons, literally the first investment bank in the United States, held a ton of Hechinger stock.

Carolyn called and asked, "Do you know anyone at Alex. Brown?"

"Yes. Yes, I do!"

A very good client of mine, Gregory Barnhill, was a vice president at Alex. Brown. He and his wife Lisa had given Designer's Hardware a lot of business and were loyal customers. If Gregory felt it appropriate, he could easily get us into Hechinger. I pitched him my idea, and he immediately saw what I was onto and agreed to help.

Two days later, I received a call from the administrative assistant to Ken Cort, the CEO of Hechinger. She asked to set up a meeting between Mr. Cort and me. I kept my cool when I said yes, but I was so giddy I nearly fainted. Carolyn and I made the trip to Landover to pitch Mr. Cort. Carolyn's husband, Richard, had been working for major corporations for years so Carolyn had deep inside knowledge of how corporations operated and what got them motivated. In our meeting with Mr. Cort, I was manic and possibly overly enthusiastic, but my zeal was just enough to be contagious. Mr. Cort listened patiently, and I could see that Carolyn and Mr. Cort had a chemistry that gave a us an advantage. We finished the pitch and shook hands.

I wasn't quite sure what he thought. He would have been a good poker player.

Mr. Cort's face then lit up, as he smiled. "Troy, this is a very intriguing notion. I think it has a lot of merit, and it's worth pursuing. I'll drop by your store in Baltimore tomorrow with our Vice President of Purchasing and Marketing, and we'll see your concept in action."

Carolyn and I had done it. We'd taken my "crazy" idea and gotten it well off the ground with a very serious suitor. We not only had found a way into Hechinger and pitched the CEO, but we'd gotten the hook so deep in his mouth, he wanted to come to our store *the next day*. Mr. Cort made the trip to our store the next day as promised and was impressed. Now. the only question now was, what kind of deal would he offer us?

Carolyn and I went back to meet with Ken Cort who was a tough negotiator as he laid out exactly what he was offering. Hechinger would commit to carving out one thousand square feet of showroom space for us, but he would not invest a dime on the build-out, displays or inventory. This expense rested solely on Designer's Hardware. That was fair. Hechinger would guarantee traffic of 80,000 people-a-month visiting the Hechinger stores, where we would be operating the concessions. That was just a little more than what our store drew. Ha, ha.

Ken asked, "What will the name of the concessions be?"

"Home Elegance," I said, without hesitation.

He considered that for a moment, then nodded. "I like it."

He told us that Hechinger's cut would be sixteen percent of our sales, in exchange for providing the space and utilities. This number was non-negotiable, but I was not surprised, considered it reasonable and readily agreed. I'd already projected in advance what a fair piece would be, and Ken's number was in the sweet spot, so I'd essentially already decided before walking into the meeting what I'd take or not. He asked if we could open our first store in three months and our second store six months after that. If the concept took off, Hechinger would want Home Elegance in thirty of their best stores over the next two years. I agreed to all his terms.

When I returned to our store, I told Arthur and Margaret about the offer—and acceptance—and the blood drained from their faces. My nutty, lame-brained idea had not only been given credibility by one of the biggest retailers in the country, but we were now in business with them. They couldn't believe what Carolyn and I had just accomplished.

But then again, what is the old saying? *Be careful what you wish for.*

***

Despite my going to all the trouble to close a deal I figured would significantly increase our bottom line, I was surprised that Arthur wanted no part of the Hechinger deal or the idea itself. He was insistent. With him out, I needed another source of cash to open two Home Elegance . We were in essence tasked with opening two new stores within six months. Albeit, they were small, but each required almost as much work and cost as the first Designer's Hardware we'd opened.

Hechinger had decided they wanted the first prototype showroom in Columbia, Maryland, an affluent, little city between Baltimore and

Washington, D.C. The second showroom would go in the pride of the entire Hechinger home center chain, a new Hechinger store in the center of Tenleytown, an upscale neighborhood in northwest Washington, D.C.

How we were going to finance these expensive little retail gems without Arthur's deep pockets was my dilemma. There was only one solution I could see. I would sell our half of Designer's Hardware to Arthur. This was the only way I could see to make my vision a reality. I bullied a pragmatic and reluctant Margaret into sharing my vision. Despite her better judgment, she could not withstand the power of her manic, bipolar husband. She also knew the business and saw the potential for it. So, the deal was set: we sold Designer's Hardware to Arthur and sunk all the money into the Home Elegance showrooms.

We went to work setting up the space, first in the Columbia, Maryland, location and then in the Tenleytown store. It cost a lot to get the look right, then to stock them both, but it was soon proven that my concept worked. We were an immediate success, and I was hailed as a retail genius by Hechinger executives and others in the home-center industry. We did more than half a million dollars in sales in less than a year, from each showroom. Home-center trade magazines did articles on our success. I was the talk of the industry and a home-center celebrity.

We were such a success that Home Depot and Lowe's sent mystery shoppers into our showrooms to study our success up close, to see if they could apply the same concepts. Hechinger was so excited by the hit on their hands, they told us they definitely wanted to move ahead with the plan to open thirty more Home Elegance showrooms in their best locations. I began actively negotiating with several national plumbing distributors to finance the two-and-a-half-dozen additional showrooms.

But there was one little problem.

Hechinger, it turned out, was in a life-and-death struggle with Home Depot and Lowe's. And they were losing. I had no idea of this dire situation when I pitched them. I'd assumed they'd been around a long time and would continue to be around, but my blind spot was the retail world at that behemoth scale. I just didn't know it, and a lot was changing. While Home Elegance was one of their few bright spots, it was not enough to keep the water from sloshing over the decks of the foundering S.S. Hechinger. Their stock was sinking with Titanic rapidity, and with growing horror, I could see the writing on the wall. The horse I'd saddled to ride turned out to be on his way to the dog food plant and not the Kentucky Derby.

Hechinger closed their doors for good in 1999. I was extremely fortunate that I did not get the financing for the thirty showrooms or I would have been royally fucked and in the tank for millions. Still, it was almost that bad. I had cashed in and given away all of our Designer's Hardware money, which was everything Margaret and I had. Thanks to the Hechinger debacle, we had only our house left to show for the last nine years of business. We'd taken our surf board to Oahu, ridden one fantastic ninety-foot wave...and then the sea got very calm. It was all over.

By then, Home Depot and Lowe's had seen the advantage of offering upscale door hardware and fancy plumbing supplies to the masses, and they sure didn't need me. Today, these categories account for a large portion of their profits. I had indeed changed an industry but had lost almost everything in the process and was lying mortally wounded in its wake. My dreams were smashed, and, despite my occasional bipolar conquer-the-world delusions, I finally had concrete, soul-crushing proof that I was but a mere mortal.

CHAPTER FIFTEEN

Zugzwang... Or Gambit Redux?

"Don't be afraid of losing, be afraid of playing a game and not learning something."
—Dan Heisman, U.S. Chess National Master

Despite Margaret's reservations and concerns about my course of action that led to our financial implosion, she continued to stand by me and keep a stiff upper lip. To her never-ending credit, she's never said *I told you so, or what the hell were you thinking?* Our heads spun as the big roller coaster of fate rolled over the top of the tracks and headed straight down, taking us from respectable business owners to lunch bag men/women nearly overnight. Margaret got a job with a local retailer to help support us, so we could maintain our health insurance. Smell that smoke? It was my reputation burning to a cinder. To the independent decorative hardware or plumbing supply companies, I was a pariah, because I'd gotten into bed with their arch-rivals, the home centers. I was the Philip Nolan of faucets, door pulls and knobs, suddenly a man without an industry.

I couldn't even get arrested in my field despite being one of the top experts in the country in the decorative door hardware-and-plumbing industry. What job was I going to get in an entirely different field with merely a ninth-grade education? People treated me like Richard Speck applying to nursing school, so I turned to the one thing I knew well that was similar to my previous career: selling home improvements. The seedy, high-pressure world I entered was right out of the classic David Mamet play and film, *Glengarry Glen Ross*. Selling home improvements on a "one-call-close" involved walking into a customer's home and, just like a game of chess, playing a sophisticated set of rules-of-engagement to effect the sale. It was you against them, and it was about as zero sum as it got. You either walked out with a yes, which was the equivalent of them laying down their king, or you leave with your tail between your legs with no sale.

Your opening moves had you first "warming them up" and getting them to like you. You'd make small talk—*Are those your kids in the picture? Nice crumb cake. I saw the bass boat in the drive. So, you're quite the fisherman, right Bob?*

It was an art form to weave a line of hollow bullshit into a narrative where you made them feel like you cared and were there to help them. As a chess player, I walked up the front walk and into the house, my eyes constantly scanning for any points of reference I could use, just as you look for weakness in another's game.

As you worked your psychological black magic and their confidence in you grew, you'd determine their needs while selling your company and building the value and solidity in your product that backed your eventual pitch. Then, once you'd established you were a force of stability and quality, you'd finally demonstrate your products as expertly as one of those pitchmen you see on TV and, as Johnny Cash sang, *"If the good Lord's willin' and the creek don't rise,"* you'd close the sale.

My selling philosophy was lean and mean and could be summarized in four words, which I repeated to myself as a mantra: *like, listen, believe, buy.* LLBB was my golden rule just as *ABC, "Always Be Closing,"* was in *Glengarry.* If they liked you, they'd listen to you. Your opening moves were designed to effect that emotion in them at all costs. Everything after that hinged on them warming to you. It was no different than lulling your chess opponent into thinking they were in much better shape than they were. If they listened to you, they'd believe you. That was now easier since you'd sort of gained their trust. If they believe you, they'd buy from you. That was when they opened their king up to attack, you cornered it with your rook and your queen, and they were toast.

Checkmate, bitch.

In those days, all the leads were telemarketing leads, because this was before the "no-call" laws that now give home owners a little added protection from that blizzard of lead-setting pests who used to flood people's phones. Telemarketing leads were nothing more than the product of rows and rows of phone solicitors in a boiler room, trying to get a home-improvement salesman's foot in the door for an estimate. If you could close one-in-three of these leads, then you were considered a good closer, and you could eke out a living. I was a very good closer.

***

One evening, I drove out to Westminster, Maryland, a small town maybe twenty-five miles outside of Baltimore. I met with a lovely, little, old lady, living alone who had to be in her late eighties. She invited me inside, and we sat down to talk. I asked her questions about her childhood, her marriages, her children, her education. I found out as much as I could, short of taking a stool sample. I just listened as she told me her entire life story in about three hours. I knew she really trusted me after that endurance run. It was almost eleven p.m., and it was either push for the close or ask where I could find the guest room.

"My goodness, look at the time! I guess I'd better show you the windows before it gets too late and I get fired," I said softly, with a smile.

Without missing a beat, she smiled back and put her hand on top of mine. "No need, dear. Let's just write up the order."

That window order came to about nineteen thousand dollars. She wrote the check and gave me a kiss on the cheek. That was a three-hour warm up and a ten-second close and paid our bills for a week or two. I also loved selling to African Americans. Hands down, their only concern was the monthly payment. If it hinged on merely extending the years of payment to get the monthly payment down to a manageable amount, you always had the sale.

"I can get you all the way down to ninety dollars a month. How does that sound?"

I'd get a thumbs up, despite them going into debt for the next three presidential terms.

The downside to home improvement sales was working nights, since you needed both decision makers present—that is, the husband and wife—and evenings were the only time the telemarketers could generally set the appointment times. This was hard on Margaret and Clara. I missed so much precious time with my daughter working nights. Margaret never complained about me being out all hours, but I knew Clara was suffering. Because of my instability and erratic behavior, I could not even keep a home-improvement job. Over the next five years, I changed jobs nine or ten times. Some of my sales managers for these home improvement companies were just like Alec Baldwin's ruthless character from *Glengarry*. Worse, sometimes.

Despite their antics and threats and carrots-on-a-stick to motivate us, they only succeeded in amusing me. Whatever they said never changed my approach of LLBB. If it worked, great. If it didn't, I'd move on, and no screaming tirades from sales managers about "burning leads" ever built a fire under me. That worked for some people, but not me. Maybe it was my feeling I was so much smarter than they were or just my stubbornness, but I did my own thing, and it usually worked. But, like a bomb with a hidden timer ticking down, I was always one misunderstanding or off-handed remark from going postal. Then, an incident in downtown Baltimore changed my life forever.

I was driving up Charles Street with Margaret in the car beside me, and we got caught behind a double-parked car. The other cars would not let me in even though my blinker was on. I tried to squeak out from behind the double-parked car and finally forced my way out by cutting off of a stubborn driver who had no intention of letting me in. I made a right turn at the next corner. The car that I had offended followed me and then managed to pull up beside me. In the car were four young black men itching for a confrontation. They made the mistake of acting aggressive and making gestures toward Margaret and me, as if I'd insulted them.

This made me go bipolar crazy. Margaret read the danger signs and tried to stop me but was too late as I rolled down my widow.

I leveled my fiercest gaze at the driver and bellowed at the top of my lungs, "What the FUCK do you want, motherfucker?"

The young man in the passenger seat seemed to express the most hostility to my comment, and his eyes challenged mine. My wild eyes were Ed Noonan death rays, directed to bore a hole through him.

"You are fucking with the wrong, motherfucking white boy, motherfucker!" I screamed at him.

He raised a gun and aimed it right at me. "I'm gonna do you, bitch!" he yelled back.

Instead of flinching as any sane person would do, I upped the ante and screamed back even louder, "Do me! Please do me, motherfucker! Just do me! I'm fucking begging you, motherfucker, go ahead and do me! Go ahead!" Then, I heard someone in the backseat warning his friends, "Fuck this crazy, white boy! He fuckin' cray-cray. Les' roll. Hit it!"

They zoomed off. I had placed my life and, likely, Margaret's life in jeopardy, but at that moment I didn't care. I didn't give a fuck, really, I wanted to die. Fuck 'em. My mind had been overtaken with rage and fury and blocked out all ability to reason and experience any other type of human emotion or normal cautions. Had Margaret *not* also died in the resulting fusillade, she would have collected the four hundred thousand in the life insurance I carried.

Win, win. She'd be set up, and I'd be out of my torment.

At least that's how my twisted logic played out at that moment. She deserved the cash for sticking by my side and tolerating all the bullshit I had put her through all those years. But the truth was that I was very comfortable as I orchestrated disaster to unfold around me, that loving embrace of the flirtation with utter and unequivocal catastrophe. It was this revelation of the magnitude of my dysfunction that caused me to finally examine how far off the path of sanity I'd strayed. I had placed Margaret's life in danger without thinking it through. I'd put Clara's father (and possibly her mother) in mortal danger, leaving to a flip of the coin whether or not she'd grow up an orphan. I'd simply reacted like a madman.

I *was* a madman. I needed help.

***

Margaret took control of helping me get well and found Marsha, a great therapist. Marsha is a Grandmaster of therapists, with a staggering wealth of experience. She listened to me, telling my life story and, after a while, she sat back in her chair and fixed her gentle eyes on me.

"Troy? You want to know what's wrong with you?"

I had to smile. It just couldn't be this easy. I was expecting her question to be a red herring or the lead-in to some kind of riddle, at which point she'd just admit I was too messed up. With years of therapy, we still might not even get to the bottom of it. I figured it was just too complicated to be summed up so soon.

"Okay," I said, "I give. What the hell's wrong with me?"

"You, Troy, are bipolar. Frankly, I'm stunned you got this far in life without this diagnosis, it's so obvious. You must have gone through a lot of pain and anxiety."

Bipolar? I sat a moment and just stared at her. *Pain and anxiety? Yes, Marsha, to put it mildly I had.*

Marsha was amazed at what I had accomplished in my life with undiagnosed bipolar. She explained that it was only because I was extremely intelligent, I had survived. Once we had unmasked my opponent and given it a name, we were able to start to piece my life back together and develop coping skills and pharmaceutical support to tame the beast. I had been playing a no-win game of chess all these years against an opponent with no name and no identity, an antagonist I thought I'd gotten a handle on but was, in fact, a malevolent ghost who'd tormented me my entire life and done so by striking from the shadows. She slowly built my self-esteem back to the point where I was ready to try and find a "real" job with real benefits that would not take me away at night from my family. Marsha referred me to a psychiatrist who prescribed Risperdal and Lamictal.

The effects were no less than miraculous.

For the first time in my life, I was stable. I didn't feel like I was a depressed, insane Clark Kent and an I-can-do-anything seemingly sane Superman. While it was true the drugs were a sort of red Kryptonite that took away my superhuman powers, they also took away the monstrous burden I'd been shouldering my entire life. It was a very happy compromise because I was no longer suicidal and destructive. I didn't have to trudge down into those despair-inducing inky-black canyons of my mind anymore. It was a damn good trade. Without the manic highs and lows, I actually started to enjoy life without feeling like there was always something better just around the bend. For the first time in my life, I realized what it was like to live like a normal person. Sure, I'd lost my X-Men powers, but you can only light so many fires with your fingertips or lift metal bridge spans with telepathy before it gets old. It was a joy to be a normal human.

CHAPTER SIXTEEN

Unpinning: A Playable Move

"These young guys are playing checkers. I'm out there playing chess."
—Kobe Bryant

Now that I was testing the new waters of normal, I had hope that getting a regular job again was a strong possibility. Rather than living on that knife's edge, as I had my whole life, I felt confident seeking some comfort and security within the conservative ranks of corporate America, an environment traditionally incompatible with wild men.

Pinning in chess is when a player makes a move that puts the other player's piece in jeopardy, but to move it out of danger requires exposing another, even more valuable piece behind it to capture. It's a tough situation. In chess, it's almost never an outcome with a happy ending, but in life, it seems, we have second chances.

In 2004, I ran across an ad for a job with Formica Corporation, the famous laminate company. The job offer was for a Specification Sales Representative who would call on architects and designers. As soon as I saw that part of the ad, I knew it was right up my alley. It also paid $55,000-a-year and, on top of that, threw in a company car, full health insurance, a laptop and an expense account.

I had to get this job. I needed this job. I could get this job.

In the 1984 song, *Please, Please, Please, Let Me Get What I Want*, the Smiths sang, "*So for once in my life let me get what I want, Lord knows, it would be the first time.*"

The first hurdle was to get past the phone interview with the recruiter. I aced it, but then my heart dropped when I heard there would be twelve finalists coming out of the phone interview stage. My chess brain instantly began calculating odds. I was given a date and time for the job interview with the Regional Manager at the Formica plant in Odenton, Maryland.

I nervously drove to Formica that afternoon and arrived at the company parking lot in my 1995 Toyota Corolla a half-hour early. I came early for a couple reasons. One was in case an asteroid hit the Earth and traffic was backed up and the other was to collect my thoughts and get my game face on for the interview. It was the end of the day, and I knew there would be only one more interview before mine. That's when I saw a brand-new Volvo wagon pull up nearby and watched as this beautiful woman in a power suit stepped out and strode confidently toward the front door.

I instantly knew Power Lady was my competition. I instantly felt like a bishop going up against a queen. Just her looks and obvious money and swagger, as she stepped across the parking lot in her spiked heels, hit me over the head that I was facing a big disadvantage before I even climbed out of my car. As she got to the door, a man rushed to open it like the servile doorman at a hotel and greeted her. The tall, thin "doorman" smiled widely at her as he lead her in, and I realized to my horror that this was the Regional Manager. By the way he fawned over Power Lady and licked her four-inch spike heels, I knew I was doomed.

The interviews were supposed to be thirty-minute blocks, but when my time came, and I went to the door to be let inside, the same tall, thin man came to the door, acting annoyed and brusquely told me to wait. I could see he was in the middle of his interview with Power Lady, and he asked me to continue to wait outside until he was through. Power Lady's interview ran a half-hour over, that is one full hour. I chalked it up as a bad sign. I wondered rather sardonically if I'd be invited to the wedding.

Finally, the Regional Manager's true love, Power Lady, skedaddled, and he was grudgingly ready for me. It was show time. I ignored the spell Power Lady may have cast and did the standard warm up that I had learned from in-home sales. I asked him about the long day of interviews he had given. I was sympathetic. I expressed concerned over his long, grueling day of sifting through applicants. I could see he was tired. I was his last interview of the day, and I sensed he wanted to get through it and get the hell out of there.

I had to ignore the fact he might have been tired, because it was my time to shine. I was going to put on the best show I could. I drew him in with questions that got him to talk about himself and used his name often, as Sigourney Weaver had taught me. Tim may have seen through my technique but didn't let on. Rather, he let me talk and then finally hit me with, "I want to see how good a salesman you are."

He took out a beautiful fountain pen from his drawer—not one you signed reports with but the fancy kind, like a Mont Blanc you only use to ink big deals. He laid it in front of me on the desk.

"Sell me this pen. Now."

I paused, gathering my thoughts and said to myself, *Troy, you got this. Use your in-home sales-selling experience to close this motherfucker!*

"Tim," I began, "what do you like best about what you're currently writing with?" "That it works well."

"Well, Tim," I continued, "what would you change, if you could, with the writing instrument you're now using?"

"Nothing. Not a thing," he said, "I like what I'm using now."

"What question should I be asking you that I am not asking you?"

He smiled. "Do I use pens?"

"Thank you, Tim. Do you use pens?"

"No."

Now I had him. I was about to say the unexpected, and I knew the power I held.

"Tim," I said, "thank you for your time, but I don't have the product in front of me to meet your needs at this time. Would you be open to seeing more options at another time?"

I wonder if his paramour Power Lady had been so audacious. A quote from somewhere in a chess book flashed through my mind: *No one has ever won a game of chess by taking only forward moves...sometimes you have to move backwards to take better steps forward.*

There was a flicker of surprise and, perhaps, a little pleasure in his eyes. He nodded. "Yes. Absolutely. I would definitely be open to that."

I had avoided the trap he had set and could tell he was impressed... but still wasn't convinced.

Maybe it was because it was the end of the day or maybe he'd already made up his mind with Power Lady, but he suddenly challenged me in a loud voice, "C'mon, Troy, DAZZLE ME!"

My expression stayed even, but I didn't really know what he wanted from me. My mind began spinning through possible reasons for this tack he'd taken. *Dazzle him? What kind of bullshit was this?* I took a slight breath and went calm. I was not going to play his game and kiss his ass. I was going to use my power and let him know who was truly in command. By doing so, if he was half the manager that I expected he was, I would get him excited that I could handle any situation I was thrown into. And, more importantly, I wanted him to feel confident I was going to make him money.

"Tim, did you read my resume?"

"Yes, I did. It was impressive."

"Thank you. Did you see that I was the top salesman at Kraft in Manhattan for four years? That I opened Designer's Hardware in Baltimore and took it from zero to two million a year in sales in three years? That I negotiated with Hechinger, a three-billion-dollar-a-year company to open an entirely new type of concession in their stores? Now, let me ask you...does any of that dazzle you?"

Maybe he was just tired. I could tell he was a little embarrassed, he had made such a thoughtless demand of someone who had spent an entire career dazzling. I think he realized it was probably more something you'd ask some twenty-year-old kid on his second job.

I looked him directly in the eyes and said, "Tim, I know you have all these candidates trying to impress you, dazzle you, if you will. It's very difficult to see into someone's heart, but this I promise you: in no time at all, I will be more valuable to Formica than Formica is to me. Does that sound reasonable, Tim?"

I knew my brazen statement struck a chord with him. In that brief moment, I knew I had a fighting chance to get the job away from Power Lady.

Or so I'd hoped.

Three days later, I received a call from Tim.

"This was one of the most difficult decisions I have ever had to make," he began, and my stomach churned. "And it came down to you and one other applicant." I knew he was talking about Power Lady. He continued, his voice tightening, "I've decided to go with her."

I was devastated. I was completely floored, so sure I had knocked it out of the park on the interview. Only the powerful medicines coursing through my system kept me from losing it. I worked hard to compose myself. *Stay classy, Troy*, I reminded myself. I took a deep breath and kept my voice calm, even cordial.

"Tim, I understand completely. If anything comes up in the future, please keep me in mind."

I wished him only the best. I had done it! With the help of medicine, I had controlled my fury and did not incinerate my bridges, nor did I go all Keyser Söze and threaten him and everyone he'd ever met. I was sooo cool.

Fortunately.

Three weeks later, Tim called me back.

"Troy, are you still interested in the job?"

It turned out Power Lady had lied on her resume about her education, and it was discovered during the vetting process. One thing I learned later was that Formica does everything first-class, and they had done so on background checks. Formica accepted me with my ninth-grade education on the condition I get my high school diploma within eighteen months. I did so within six. I attended the South Baltimore Learning Center on Ostend Street and came away with a State of Maryland high school diploma.

And I'll bet Power Lady was behind on her Volvo payments, too.

CHAPTER SEVENTEEN

Clara

"You will never have this day with your children again. Tomorrow they'll be a little older than they were today. This day is a gift. Just breathe, notice, study their faces and little feet. Pay attention. Relish the charms of the present. Enjoy today, it will be over before you know it."
—Jen Hatmaker

I have used chess analogies for every chapter until now. On the chess board, all of the pieces have the singular duty of protecting the king and defeating the other side. In life, it turns out, there is a piece or pieces that transcend the importance of the king, queen and all the rest and yet there is nothing analogous in chess: children. You bring them into the world, hopefully in love, and you nurture them like fragile flowers in your own little garden. Then, one day, they take their place in the bigger garden of the world. You hope, you pray that they are ready and will thrive. Your dreams for your children rise and fall with their every step or misstep. The first word, the first tooth, the first time they call you mommy or daddy. All moments etched in your heart.

Clara was a sweet little girl. She was a happy child, outgoing and funny. While she never had a large circle of friends, she seemed to enjoy other kids but tended to gravitate toward the quieter ones like herself.

She also enjoyed one-on-one play as opposed to groups of other kids. Another characteristic Margaret and I found interesting was that she preferred making friends with boys instead of girls.

We soon began to see our little girl was not like most other kids. Even as a toddler, less than four years old, she began quoting lines from movies. She became a movie buff from the get-go and quickly passed *Beauty and The Beast* and graduated to films with adult, far-more-complex themes and plot structures. Not quite Federico Fellini—yet—but way out of the range of most kids. She devoured movies like a starved person. Films seemed to stimulate her wildly-encompassing imagination and intellect in a way other pastime, save for reading, did not. We would notice her explaining to her playmates the nuanced story development of films that they didn't seem to grasp. It was like watching a seven-year-old teach film theory or story structure.

We found it oddly amusing, and because of that and other advanced personality traits, Margaret and I began treating her more like an adult than a child. Speaking to her as a child almost seemed as if we were patronizing her. It was weird, but we rolled with it. Clara exhibited other forms of her vivid imagination, playing in her head and inventing games and play that soon began to distance her from other kids who eventually just couldn't keep up. Clara was also a super-sensitive kid who evinced some troubling signs early on. She began to dedicate time almost every day to bouts of crying as if looking for some kind of release. While it got our attention, we didn't really see it as a red flag. Yet. However, we both noticed early on that the world just seemed to overwhelm our Clara.

Margaret and I developed a habit every weekend of leaving Clara with Margaret's mother, Giulia, whom she called Nonna. This gave Margaret and me time for ourselves, but in retrospect the impact of Clara and Nonna spending so much time together ,was likely significant but is hard to determine. While Nonna was very loving and gave great care, she had a particular worldview that had been forged in the fires of war and strife. I'm afraid that Nonna's well intentioned old-country, tough-love ethos tended to undermine fragile Clara's self-esteem by giving her little to no praise and fixating on her weaknesses. While I believe Nonna meant well by stressing failings, as moments to grow and improve, for a child as tuned to an almost hyperreality as Clara, her grandmother's incessant nitpicking was so jarring, this exposure to negative reinforcement may have had a more profound, injuring effect on her than we ever imagined.

At five, Clara was diagnosed with ADHD.

I admit I also didn't help cradle Clara as much as I probably should have. A bit of a prodigy, I taught her to play chess at around three—hello, Mozart—and by six or so she could beat most adults. She seemed to spark to it and showed the same ability as her father to look deep into a game and create a long-term strategy. I was delighted my child was so good but sadly my bipolar proclivities would come to ruin a good thing.

One day, when she was around eight, we were playing a game, and she made an obvious blunder and lost. I snapped. I went ballistic. On an eight-year-old. I berated her for such a careless mistake. But my words cut deep into her delicate psyche, and she walked away from chess and never played again.

When she began school in the first grade, we enrolled her at Ruxton Country School in Owings Mills, Maryland. We chose Ruxton because of the small class sizes, and so did many parents of children with ADHD. By the fourth grade, she began to develop behavioral issues caused by mean-spirited children who delighted in tormenting her because of her reserved personality and exceptional intelligence. Kids can be cruel. The bullying at school merely served to set her further apart from the other kids and magnified her loneliness and sadness.

My having to work day-and-night, setting up and running Home Elegance, also affected her, because she missed me and had a longing for time with her dad. Margaret filled the void as best she could do. Clara loved being with her mom who was always a good listener and lovingly non-judgmental. Clara was a delicate flower that required extra care and attention. lest it wilt.

She started experiencing bouts of depression by the fourth grade. She wasn't yet ten. She began seeing a therapist for support and to develop social skills that would help align her with other students, but Clara was always a square peg in a round hole. While she was so friable, I believe there was some of me and even a little bit of Granddaddy Noonan along with some of her tough European stock within her. Combined with her inordinate brain power, it was quite difficult to mold her to fit a standard. Clara, like the rest of our line, has always been her own person, and you had to accept her on her own terms. This was also about the time I was diagnosed with bipolar. While I had my answer, Clara would not be diagnosed as such until she was seventeen.

In the sixth grade, Clara made a new discovery that opened an exciting vista for her: acting. Having been a devotee of film since she could barely speak, acting suddenly became a revelation for her. She could not only do it but showed immediate promise. As a sixth grader, she got a speaking role in an eighth-grade play and impressed everyone with her talent. With that, her acting career was off to a start. She would maintain her love of acting for quite a few years.

But, sadly, by the seventh grade, Clara was back in such distress, she began cutting herself with a box knife to relieve tension. Known as non-suicidal self injury, cutting, according to those who do it, is a way to actually feel alive and escape the numbness they feel, the suffocating ennui of their lives. Over the summer, before eighth grade, she became obsessed with her weight and eating habits and started restricting her intake of food. She was already thin but not unhealthy. She soon remedied that. By fall, she had simply quit eating and the war with anorexia was upon us. When she withered away to less than seventy-eight pounds, we had her hospitalized at the Center for Eating Disorders at Sheppard Pratt in Towson, Maryland. Over the next few years, she was admitted two additional times to Sheppard Pratt to control her anorexia.

Her first hospitalization was the during the winter Formica hired me. My company insurance policy was literally activated just three days before her admission into the Center for Eating Disorders. That timing was rather miraculous as we would not have been able to afford her very expensive hospitalization otherwise. Margaret and I shared the intense pain of seeing our little girl in such agony. Anorexia is quite cruel in that it robs the sufferer of all of their motivation for anything other than the single-minded focus on weight and the less the better. They also become blind to their own appearance, seeing a hollowed-out, desiccated body as bloated and obese. It's one of the more pernicious tricks the mind is capable of playing on itself.

Despite her burdens, Clara did become a pretty good actress, in demand for student plays. She earned another feather in her cap when she was accepted by Bryn Mawr, the elite school for girls in Baltimore, ranked number six for girls' schools in the United States. No girl from Ruxton Country School had ever been accepted to Bryn Mawr. She would be going to one of the most rigorous curricula in the country. Many of Baltimore's elite families sent their children to Bryn Mawr. It cost in excess of $20,000-a-year to send your child there, which would have been way out of our league, but along with Clara getting a generous scholarship and Margaret's mother paying the balance, she made it in the doors.

Despite the excitement of getting her into such an august institution, the same old problems plagued her. Her eccentricities made it hard for her to make friends with the students at Bryn Mawr. She chose to ignore that and threw herself into acting. She plated Kira in *Gathering Blue* and had roles in the classics, *School for Scandal* and *Much Ado About Nothing*. She even moved up from student productions to regional theater with *Clue: The Musical* at the Spotlighters Theater in downtown Baltimore.

She was an incredibly gifted actress, and we were extremely proud of her. We hoped against hope that she'd turned a corner, and it would be smooth sailing for her.

We sent her up to Philadelphia to The University of the Arts for a summer-long acting school. We were thrilled she had gotten into such a prestigious school, but our delight was short-lived. While there, she had her first major bout of bipolar mania and started cutting herself again. The school's administration couldn't be responsible for anyone who committed self-mutilation, especially a minor, so they threw her out of acting school. That was when she lost interest and gave up acting altogether, although to this day she admits she still harbors an interest in the arts.

It's a testament to Clara's intelligence she made it through four years of Bryn Mawr suffering from ADHD, bipolar and anorexia. Clara is an intellect, and she's managed to absorb a large catalogue of things artistic. She has read more than 500 books and has seen a staggering number of movies, although her taste runs to the esoteric and quite dark. She's more drawn to David Lynch than Woody Allen. She has a stunning library of films in her head that includes everything from the storylines to the best dialogue from each.

Clara went on to Goucher College, and after the rigorous curriculum at Bryn Mawr, it was a breeze, with her graduating cum laude after barely applying herself.

While at Goucher, Clara started smoking pot. Any psychotropics for someone with bipolar can be dangerous, even something as benign as dope. You are always looking to deal better with your mood, your high, your job, your relationship, your life. Studies have shown that cannabis can induce psychosis and, at the very least, anxiety, in a psychiatric patient, while others say that it can have beneficial effects for someone with bipolar. It didn't matter, since she moved away from that quickly after a boyfriend introduced her to cocaine. For someone who was bipolar, the nitromethane jolt from coke was like substituting Evil Knievel's motorcycle with a rocket launcher. Jeopardy ensues, guaranteed.

Clara was accepted to graduate school at Johns Hopkins University in non-fiction writing. While in grad school, Clara moved up from coke to mood hammers, like Percocet and OxyContin, which are simply brand names for the powerful opioid oxycodone. Then it was a simple jump to heroin. How she made it through graduate school at Johns

Hopkins and earned her master's degree while strung out on heroin is beyond my ken.

Since she received her degree, we've had to put Clara into rehab at least four times and twice into halfway houses. She has been hospitalized nine times for suicidal ideation or attempts, trying to kill herself. Somewhere along the line, she turned to the Mack Daddy of self-destructive drugs, methamphetamine (and yes, I'm not counting the insanity of desomorphine, a.k.a. Krokodil, which is simply a vehicle to commit a slow and ghastly suicide). While meth is used to control ADHD and has its uses, for sure, as a recreational drug, its lethality and ability to destroy one's life is legendary...and documented. Thankfully, she finally stopped that, because she became psychotic and feared that, once she crossed that Rubicon, there really might not be a return to sanity.

She's now on Suboxone, a prescription drug that treats addiction, and we have been able to wean her off heroin. Still, she has a slip now and then, taking Xanax, a pretty potent sedative. We are always hopeful, but it's been an ordeal, for her and us. Throughout these years, Margaret and I have never felt we were really living, just surviving. To have your baby, your only child, in such pain, going through such a living hell, is sometimes just impossible to take. But we find a way and keep moving.

There is a beam of hope, as Clara has turned out to be a gifted writer. She gave up acting and still loves films, but her new passion is the word on the page. She's a frenetic journaler and dutifully keeps a running record of her thoughts and observations. She's been published in *Adelaide Literary Magazine*, the literary journal *trampset* and *Clamp mag*. She is currently writing a book about being bipolar and growing up with a bipolar parent.

Margaret and I aren't religious people, but we sure pray for Clara to achieve some sort of stability and blossom into the powerhouse talent—and happy, joyous person—we know she can be.

EPILOGUE

Making It Across the Board

"After the game, the king and the pawn go into the same box."
—*Italian proverb*

I have been teaching chess for the past ten years but playing very little tournament chess. Several of my scholastic students have been ranked in the top one hundred for their age group in the U.S. My adult students include a CEO, a therapist and other professionals. Around 2006, I experienced a revelation when I discovered two chess-opening repertoire books by Roman Dzindzichashvili, the aforementioned Georgian Grandmaster from the former USSR. In 1976, he left the Soviet Union for Israel, and then immigrated to the United States. Roman has won the United States Chess Championship twice, is a well-known and highly-respected chess-opening theoretician, as well as a legendary speed-blitz player. (He was a second for Gata Kamsky and Viktor Korchnoi, and many Grandmasters pay him for his opening analyses.)

As with almost all tournament chess players, I had been searching for the Holy Grail of chess-opening repertoire for almost 45 years. In his books, I thought I finally found my answers, two 500-plus-page volumes for both the white and black players, *Chess Openings for White,*

Explained and *Chess Openings for Black, Explained*. It sounds insane to a non-chess player to somehow devote a thousand pages to openings for both white and black pieces, but believe me, they are mind-blowing for me. Dzindzi also produced dozens of DVDs on his repertoire.

I went all in and purchased his books and all of his DVDs. I became a Dzindzi disciple. As someone with bipolar, I proceeded to read each book six times. I must be a blast at parties, huh? Who else but a bipolar chess player would read such books six times each and memorize them? I became an authority on his recommended opening repertoire. I found out Dzindzi's mother lived in Arlington, Virginia, and whenever he visited her from Boston, I paid three hundred dollars for private lessons on his repertoire. Some people love Elvis. Some are Beliebers. I was a Dzindziphile.

I gave his repertoire a spin in the 2007 Baltimore Open and came in second, undefeated behind Estonian Grandmaster Jaan Elhvest. I played Board One for the Catonsville Chess Club in the 2009 United States Amateur Team Championship and also went undefeated.

I played in the 2011 Maryland Senior Championship, and although I came in third place, I was again undefeated. This was a total of 15 rated tournament chess games against International Masters, Masters, Candidate Masters, Class A and Class B players, all the while using Dzindzi's amazing opening repertoire for a total of six wins and nine draws.

As you can see, as I have gotten older, I am more susceptible to draws. Maybe I don't have that kill 'em bloodlust fired by unchecked bipolar I used to have. Unfortunately, I've since found some surprising holes in the Dzindzi's repertoire and have given it up. I'm no longer a Dzindziphile. Go figure.

I am now in a phase that my best friend Mike Ladzinski calls "spin dry," continuing my search again for the Rosetta Stone of chess repertoires. While my search continues, my job with Formica is solid, my wife is happy, my daughter is seeking the best care and looking forward to scaling the K2 of literature and I'm managing to maintain an even strain with my medicine. I've been at Formica for fifteen years. In years past, even 15 weeks seemed like a long time, so I'm deeply grateful for the stability I know today, being able to enjoy a so-called normal life.

I call on architects and designers and believe that some of the smartest, classiest people in the world are in that design community. I give product and Continuing Education Unit presentations, quote prices, update design libraries, project track, and assist national account selling. I'm delighted to have that job and love my work.

And I haven't threatened any human being's life in many years. Whew!

***

Margaret has been happy I've been able to walk the straight and narrow with nary an incident. I owe everything to her for standing beside me all these years and making me seek help. I plan to pay back her devotion and forbearance with loyalty and love for the next twenty years.

At least.

"I leave this to you."
—Bobby Fischer

About the Author

Troy Roberts is the author of *Next Move: My Terrible, Wonderful, Bipolar Life*, his first book. Raised in a Baltimore family with mob ties, he grew up in a tumultuous household, surrounded by crime, prostitution, violence and drugs, often escaping with his mother and sister to his grandparent's home near Savannah, Georgia. As an early teen, he fell under the thrall of the Jehovah's Witnesses, but by the time he was in his mid- teens he found another, far more powerful obsession: chess. Despite an almost crippling affliction of bipolar inherited from both sides of his family, he managed to rise from his circumstances and become a top-rated U.S. chess player, achieving the rank of Life Master. Professionally, he was the brains behind the rise of high-end designer hardware and plumbing fixtures in big box retailers such as Lowe's and Home Depot. He calls Baltimore home and lives in the area with his wife and daughter. He still plays and teaches chess. He can be reached at callsophie@verizon.net.

Apprentice
House Press
Loyola University Maryland

Apprentice House is the country's only campus-based, student-staffed book publishing company. Directed by professors and industry professionals, it is a nonprofit activity of the Communication Department at Loyola University Maryland.

Using state-of-the-art technology and an experiential learning model of education, Apprentice House publishes books in untraditional ways. This dual responsibility as publishers and educators creates an unprecedented collaborative environment among faculty and students, while teaching tomorrow's editors, designers, and marketers.

Outside of class, progress on book projects is carried forth by the AH Book Publishing Club, a co-curricular campus organization supported by Loyola University Maryland's Office of Student Activities.

Eclectic and provocative, Apprentice House titles intend to entertain as well as spark dialogue on a variety of topics. Financial contributions to sustain the press's work are welcomed. Contributions are tax deductible to the fullest extent allowed by the IRS.

To learn more about Apprentice House books or to obtain submission guidelines, please visit www.apprenticehouse.com.

Apprentice House
Communication Department
Loyola University Maryland
4501 N. Charles Street
Baltimore, MD 21210
Ph: 410-617-5265 • Fax: 410-617-2198
info@apprenticehouse.com • www.apprenticehouse.com

CPSIA information can be obtained
at www.ICGtesting.com
Printed in the USA
LVHW081813240222
711930LV00004B/309